WARRIOR

How I survived child sexual abuse and built
the first world-class treatment centre for kids
who have been sexually abused

GLORI MELDRUM

Glori Meldrum

ISBN: 9798551699842

DEDICATION

I dedicate this book to the love of my life, my husband, Gary. He taught me how to love, how to be a mom, and how to be a caring human. He is the greatest gift I've received. Thank you, Gary.

I dedicate this book to all little warriors. I believe in your healing and I believe in you.

IN APPRECIATION

Warrior is shared with love, grace, and in the spirit of knowing that people are doing the best they can. I've come a long way from anger and hate. *Warrior* is a memoir of my abuse and journey to healing. It's taken me over five years to get the story out of my memories and into black and white. The process hasn't been easy, and many times I had to lay aside the work because the triggers and flashbacks were overwhelming. My heart and soul are in this book. Above all, I've laboured to be respectful and honouring to family members and others in my journey. Please don't hold it against people for the ways they behaved. This is the truth about my abuse and healing, not judgment. The names of many people have been changed out of respect for them.

My mom only wanted good for her daughters and did her very best for us, often to her detriment. My story can't be told without you, Mom. Thank you, Dad for always believing in me especially when I doubted myself. You taught me to dream big.

Eileen LaBonte is my second mom. Eileen, you helped my dreams come true and created an incredible legacy for children through Be Brave Ranch. You know how much I love you. Thank you.

To the Little Warriors Board of Directors, staff and everyone at g[squared], you are family to me. I am so grateful and proud of all we've accomplished together.

Where do I begin to say thanks to everyone who believed in us and supported us? There are some supporters named in this book, but it would take a dozen books to tell all the stories of your kindnesses. Thank you. Thank you. Thank you. You helped my dream come true and to leave a legacy of healing for kids who were sexually abused. I love you.

PRAISE FOR WARRIOR

"I used to believe that growth after trauma was some kind of consolation prize, a cruel joke of fate. It's not until we are at our lowest, that we are confronted with life's most dynamic choice—to recoil or to persevere. But Glori shows us there is another more nourishing path, the ability to surrender and fall gracefully into the lessons and truths that echo in the depths of our trauma and adversity. Over the years, Glori has shown us all that being brave has little to do with brute strength or willpower, and everything to do with our ability to find comfort in vulnerability, to seek out authentic connection and to find hope in steadfast honesty."

— *Jean-Paul Bédard, Elite athlete, author*

"A raw, gut-wrenching and empowering read about a life that is violated at a young age, yet rises from the depths of despair to reach heights of success most can only dream of. This story is bravely told and needs to be read and shared. Glori redefines authenticity in how she recounts the details of her life and the difficult moments that contributed to the person she is today. Glori's memoir took me there in every capacity. Reading it, I felt as though she was sitting beside me, telling me her story. Glori is the definition of what 'being brave' is all about."

— *Carrie Doll, The Inner Circle*

"From Glori's most painful and vulnerable experiences remarkable compassion was born. Her work for others is inspiring to all who know her."

— *Amanda Lindhout, Author,*
A House In The Sky, New York Times bestseller

"Reading *Warrior* makes me want to give Glori a huge hug. I didn't just read the book; I lived so many emotional experiences with her. Thank you for sharing your story and inspiring so many to fight for what is needed. I am truly in awe of what you created at Be Brave Ranch. We need more warriors like you in our society. We all have it in ourselves to surrender our pain to God and let him lead us to our fullest potential."

— *Lynne Rosychuk, Founder of the Jessica Martel Foundation*
Lynne's daughter, Jessica, was murdered by
her abusive husband in 2009

"After reading *Warrior*, I owe Glori a debt of gratitude. This book changed my life. I started my journey of healing because of *Warrior*. This is not a book about trauma; it's a pathway to healing and Glori inspired me to do the work to heal."

— *Sage Watson, Canadian record holder in the 400m hurdles;*
2016 Canadian Olympic Team member

"Reading *Warrior* took me through a journey of reflection and praise to Glori Meldrum for the strength, courage and resilience she has endured and thoughtfully writes about. *Warrior* will open your heart, mind and soul of how sexual abuse affects children and provides hope with the recovery and healing that can occur with the proper resources and supports. I had the pleasure of meeting Glori in 2016, which included a tour of the Be Brave Ranch. Glori and her team of Warriors are to be applauded for creating a safe haven for healing and positive change, and for teaching children who have been traumatized that they are loved."

— Carol Todd, Amanda Todd Legacy Society
Carol's daughter, Amanda, died by suicide in 2012,
after enduring years of merciless cyber-bullying

"Sometimes, we are handed a scenario that was not what we had planned for our life. My life scenario, unfortunately, was not at all what my husband and I had planned. In January 2015, after losing my husband to murder, I was blessed with being introduced to Glori, who quickly became a dear friend and someone who I now refer to as one of my Angels. Glori came into my life at a time when I needed to know that even after a tragedy, there still can be a life of happiness, love and most of all belief. Glori has taught everyone through this book that no matter what life throws at us that we can surpass it and walk out as a Warrior! *Warrior* pulls you in to see the reality of the abuse and how she pulled herself from the offramp of life and turned things around to help others who have been faced with monsters in their life. It also shows us all it is ok to be vulnerable, how we have to keep believing in faith and that it is ok to ask for help. I invite you to take the time to read this amazing book, as Glori opens her heart, emotions and gets real about life and how we can become a warriors."

— Shelly MacInnis-Wynn, widow of slain
RCMP Constable, David Wynn

TABLE OF CONTENTS

INTRODUCTION

I'm a survivor of childhood trauma, just like Glori Meldrum.

In 2009 Glori reached out to me and shared her story. I was intrigued by what she was trying to accomplish. She's relentless and tenacious, and very rarely do I find those qualities in a survivor of sexual abuse. She gets the concept that helping is healing. In the field of childhood trauma, you need compassion, empathy and sympathy. That's Glori. I was knocked over by her enthusiasm and energy for helping survivors of abuse.

My abuse started as far back as I can remember. Everybody focuses on what happened to me as an adolescent with a coach, but both my parents struggled with personal addictions in their life. I saw a lot of things that a young child shouldn't see.

My hockey coach sexually molested me over a 150 times. The abuse went on for over two and a half years. The reason I didn't say anything was I wanted to be an NHL hockey player. This particular coach held my career in the palm of his hand. I trusted him. Everybody did. When I told my story, everything blew up. Even today I'm still looked at as somebody who blew the whistle on a subject that an organization like the Western Hockey League doesn't want to talk about.

All the negative issues we have in society start with childhood trauma. All that's left is choosing your poison—alcohol, sex, drugs, gambling, food, or becoming a workaholic. Pain manifests itself in diseases such as mental health, anxiety/panic disorder and more.

You get to a point in this process where you have to make a choice. Am I going to die or am I going to live? On September 18, 2005 I made a choice to stop using drugs and alcohol to deal with the pain of my past. I got honest and open and told the world my story. Coming forward and talking about the secrets was when my breakthrough happened. Instead of feeling shame I felt empowered.

In 2009, when my book *Playing With Fire* was released, I had my first book signing at the Eaton Centre in Toronto. Four hundred people showed up. Out of the corner of my eye I spotted a guy. He had my book very close to his chest. His gaze was focused on the floor. When he got to the front of the line he put my book on the table, looked me in the eye and said, "Me too." That was the day I found the purpose for my life—to help other people by sharing my story and my experience.

I've never been much of a reader, but I discovered that books change people's thinking and change their lives. That's why I'm so happy Glori got her story down on paper. Glori's survival and perseverance needs to be heard across North America because not many people want to talk about the subject. Eighty percent of survivors of child sexual abuse end up being outcasts from their own family. Not many families want sexual abuse to be talked about. Glori's own family sided with her abuser so they could sweep the pain under the carpet and pretend it didn't happen. Even if people refuse to believe a survivor's story, sharing is when the healing starts. We are only as sick as our secrets. For someone to be that brave and bring it to the forefront shows others that they can do it too for their own sake. And her story is not just about the abuse. Her story is about the courage she showed to make something of her life and give back by starting Little Warriors and building the Be Brave Ranch. Her example shows kids that no matter what they've gone through they can make something good out of their lives.

Every minute of the day there is some boy or girl being abused somewhere in Canada. Think about that. Think of all the hurt that is out there. I helped set up a foundation—Breaking Free

Foundation. We're all about healing the hurts of people. We want to shift people from thinking they are victims of trauma to a place where they see themselves as survivors. When a person can reach their full potential that's a powerful tool for healing. So I teach people about self-forgiveness and self-love.

One of our organization's purposes is to raise money for Little Warriors and the Be Brave Ranch. I wish there was a Be Brave Ranch there for me. The sooner a child can get into care and treatment the better chance they have of healing. I was 41 when I first told my story. My abuse started when I was a teen. Think of all the pain and wreckage that could have been dealt with earlier if there was help for me as a kid.

It took me 27 years to feel comfortable in my own skin. That's why Glori's work through Little Warriors and Be Brave Ranch is so important to me and has a huge place in my heart and soul. The more places we have like the Ranch, the more places people can go to and heal and go on to live happy, healthy and productive lives.

At the end of the day, God picked me and God picked Glori. He knew that we would find the strength to get through what we needed to get through. I am feeling very blessed that there are people like myself and Glori, who are making a difference in the lives of kids. She's sharing her story to show survivors discover they don't have to be defined by their past. Giving kids a different life from what Glori and I had is what its all about.

I don't like surprises but when Glori showed me the hockey rink at Be Brave Ranch I was humbled. Hockey was my happy place. Then it became my unhappy place. I was incredibly honoured to have the rink at the Be Brave Ranch named after me. I shed a few tears that day. The "Theo Fleury Rink of Courage" will probably host a few battles of Alberta. And how ironic is it that there is a rink with my name on it near Edmonton, of all places?

Thank you, Glori, for writing your story. You need to hear that from me, because you'll also hear it from other people.

After you read this book, share it with the people in your life. Get behind the healing that is happening at Be Brave.

Theo Fleury, #14

PROLOGUE

I'm a survivor.

I'm strong... I'm weak... I'm confident... I'm afraid... I laugh... I cry... I hide... I walk in the sunshine.

I was a victim.

Today, I'm a survivor.

I'm on a journey of healing, with its twists and turns, highs and lows. I have good days and bad days. But each time I stumble, I pick myself up and take the next step.

I'm human.

I'm a Warrior.

CHAPTER 1
THE MONSTER

"Though I walk through the valley of the shadow of death."

— Psalm 23

———

My mom sighed as I walked into the living room and turned her attention from the black-and-white television screen.

"Look at you, Glori. You're filthy."

Praying she would turn her attention from me and back to the TV show, I didn't say a thing. There was no denying it. A week's worth of grime covered every inch of my eight-year-old body, and even I wasn't immune to the odour.

"You need a bath."

My strategy wasn't working.

"Now."

I pretended not to hear her.

"That's a good TV show," I said, pointing to the television, but she was too smart to be fooled by such an obvious trick.

"Don't change the subject," she said. "You're taking a bath."

I looked down at the floor. "I don't want to," I whispered.

"I don't care if you don't want to. You're going to take one and that's that."

"I don't want to," I repeated quietly.

"What's the matter with you? You never were like this before."

I looked up and wanted to tell her. I needed to tell her. But then I remembered the promise made to my step-grandfather in his car. The thought of it made me burst into tears. Ashamed, I turned and ran away.

"Glori, get back here!" she shouted after me.

I kept running until I reached the space under the basement stairs. This was my hiding place. My secret. Or so my eight-year-old mind imagined. It was where I went when I didn't know what to do; a last resort. Dark, cold, cramped and certainly not comfortable in the least, but it was better than the monster finding me. Some kids are afraid of imaginary monsters because of the dark. I was terrified it wasn't dark enough to keep the monster from finding me.

I made myself as quiet as possible, only taking short little breaths to remain completely silent. In the stillness I could make out the voices of the adults upstairs. They were talking about me.

"I don't know what's wrong with her," I heard my mom complain. "She's been such a pain lately."

"It's just a phase," my grandmother told her. "All kids go through something like it. Isn't that right, Wib?"

Wib just grunted. My step-grandfather knew why I didn't want to take a bath.

There was nothing I could do but wait and hope that when I finally left my hiding place, my mom would have forgotten all about the bath I desperately needed. "If I can just put it off until tomorrow," I thought. Surviving each day was my biggest concern.

Minutes felt like hours, especially when I realized that I had to go to the bathroom. I ignored the creeping sensation for a little while, but soon, my bladder's gentle request turned into an angry demand. I tried holding my breath, but that only made it worse.

Tears welled up in my eyes. I only had two choices—leave my hiding place and get caught or go in my pants like a baby.

I've since learned that when a child starts wetting themselves long after potty training, it's often a sign that abuse has taken place. I can relate to those kids. I hated going to the bathroom for fear of abuse. The choice of peeing my pants or running upstairs wasn't clear. I had to think about it. On a different day, I might have chosen to soil myself, but this day, I decided I couldn't abandon my dignity. I wouldn't let Wib turn me into a baby.

Crawling out of my hiding space, I sprinted to the bathroom. I was always a fast runner, but at that moment I could have won Olympic gold. The bathroom was empty, and I had just enough time to close the door and pull my pants down before wetting myself.

"Gotcha!" the door burst open. The lock was broken. Wib fixed most things around the house, but not the bathroom lock. I screamed from the surprise and almost fell off the toilet. It was my mom, looking victorious.

"Get undressed," she ordered as she turned on the taps to the tub.

I finished peeing and did as I was told. For a moment, I considered throwing a tantrum, but by now, I was too tired to yell or fight. I dipped a toe into the tub and winced. My mom saw this and dipped a finger in to see if I was faking.

"Sorry, sweetie," she apologized as she turned off the hot water and let the cold run for a little longer.

I stepped back into the tub and sat down. The water was now comfortably lukewarm, and I had to admit it felt wonderful against my skin.

"Now scrub," my mom demanded with a bar of soap in her hand.

I grabbed the soap and started scrubbing. My mom stood up and turned towards the door.

"Please don't go," I pleaded with her.

"What is wrong with you?"

"I just want you to stay."

"That's sweet, Glori," she smiled at me, "but I have things to do, and big girls have to take baths by themselves."

"I don't want to be a big girl," I told her.

"Too late," she laughed as she tousled my hair. "Don't forget to wash behind your ears," she added before she turned around and walked out the door.

With her gone, I knew I had to get myself clean as quickly as I could. I scrubbed so hard it turned my skin red. Maybe if I did it fast enough, I could get out safely.

The door opened.

I held my breath, hoping to see my mother's face, but it was the monster in her place.

CHAPTER 2

JOY AND INNOCENCE

"The miracle of children is that we just don't know how they will change or who they will become."

— *Eileen Kennedy-Moore*

My Mom and Dad, Clyde and Iva

Mom had 50 cents in her pocket when she jumped in a taxi to leave my dad. The cab fare from Chatham, New Brunswick to her mother's house in Miramichi was $2.50, so she borrowed the difference from her mom. It was 1975. I was two years old, my sister Bobbie was a newborn and the drama had officially started.

I was so young when my parents separated that I have very few memories of them as a couple. Were it not for the handful of photographs of the two of them I'm not sure I could tell you what might have drawn them together. From the photos, I surmised it must have been a physical attraction.

My dad, Clyde, could have been a member of The Guess Who or some other rock band from the era. Like all of the men she dated, my dad exuded strength and had a quick temper. Plus, he had a killer moustache.

My mom, Iva, was a thin, dark-haired and fragile beauty. She had long legs that she showed off in short skirts and tight shorts. When she later dyed her hair blonde, she resembled a harsher, angrier version of Mia Farrow. Despite her fierce expression, she had a submissive personality that often took her into the arms of domineering men.

Their relationship lasted just barely long enough to produce Bobbie and me. I was born in the spring of 1973, and Bobbie arrived at the end of summer in 1975. Mom's expensive cab ride came not long after that. We lived in Miramichi for about a year, staying in a one-storey house on MacIntosh Street.

Small-town New Brunswick wasn't the most hospitable place for a single mother in the mid-1970s. Unable to find a job to support us, my mom reached out to her sisters in British Columbia. They convinced her to move the three of us across the country to live near them where they could all attempt to make it together. Mom's sister Nancy paid our airfare.

With nothing to lose, my mom left her old life behind and traveled more than 3,500 miles with two young kids and $54 in her pocket.

Settling in Vancouver, we lived with my Aunt Nancy and her then-boyfriend, Ted. Six months later we moved to Port Coquitlam to live in a house we shared with Mom's other sister, Elsie. Nancy soon followed us, as did another sister, Fern and new boyfriend Alfie.

The living conditions were cramped.

The Bad Men

During my early years in B.C., Fern and Nancy would play essential roles in my young life. They filled in the gaps for my mom wherever needed. Fern, the youngest sibling, was a nurturer who often babysat us, while Nancy was a vivacious blond with a string of sugar daddies. These men provided her with the means to spoil us with presents that our mom would never have been able to afford.

I went to Aunt Fern when I needed a hug.

Aunt Nancy bought me my first bike.

Mom got a job working as a collections officer. Her boss started dating her right away. Almost as quickly, we had a new roommate in our cramped little house. For some reason, Mom never dated guys with houses big enough for us all.

Her boss was a tall, broad-shouldered, muscular guy named Mike, and he was a total jerk. I suppose his demeanor must have served him well as a collections officer, but it didn't leave a good impression on Bobbie and me. His green eyes were his most endearing feature. He sometimes sported a beard with matching light brown shoulder-length hair and a wrinkled face. When he was in the room, he was the boss.

I never liked Mike from the moment we met. I never liked any of Mom's boyfriends. Each new guy meant Bobbie and I got shunted to the back seat.

My only good memory of Mike involved him and Alfie building the "some construction required" pink Barbie Campervan I received for Christmas that year. Other than that, he was a textbook example of the kind of guy a young mother should never bring home to her kids.

Despite our poverty, Mom had established every Friday as a treat day. When she had cash, this meant going to a budget-conscious fast food place like McDonald's or A&W (and if we were fortunate, the International House of Pancakes). Even when she was broke, she'd scrape together enough change to bring home a box of Twinkies or doughnuts, making sure we always celebrated the weekend's arrival.

Mom has always had a beautiful and kind heart in spite of her weaknesses. She did the best with what she had, and back in those days, she didn't have much. The ritual of a Friday night treat was one of the many ways she showed love.

Another of my favourite memories is collecting rocks with my mom. She took me out collecting regularly, and if you think about it, rock collecting is a genius way to create meaning and memories between mother and daughter when there is no money. Rocks lying on beaches, in the hills and on mountain trails are free. Each one is different, and even if you don't understand the geology of the rock, each one tells a story. I still love rocks today. I keep collections of them in my home and office, and I'm always on the search for new, meaningful stones. I even give them as gifts.

Like so many women, my mom's sense of weakness consumed her. I would later learn there was a reason for her poor choices. To combat her insecurity, she sought the company of stereotypically macho men in the misguided belief that their "manliness" would protect her. Attracted to the aura of potential violence that emanated from such men, she was oblivious to the reality that this violence was likely to be directed at us.

In Mike's case, this became evident one night while she was out. Her absence peeved him. Bobbie and I were sleeping when he burst into our room. The door slammed against the wall and woke us up immediately. Too shocked to be scared, we stared, as he stood there, red-faced and puffing like some machete-wielding maniac in a bad 1980's slasher movie.

Fortunately, Aunt Fern heard the commotion. She rushed from her adjacent bedroom, ran past him and scooped both of us into her arms, and jumped out of his way as he lunged at us. She got past him and ran into her room, locked the door and jammed a chair under the doorknob.

BAM!

BAM!

BAM!

The room shook as he pounded his fists against the door. Aunt Fern had a frog figurine collection in her room. Hundreds of them adorned her bureau, dresser and end tabletops. I remember seeing the frogs tremble and dozens of them fell noisily off the dresser onto the floor. Bobbie started crying. Aunt Fern held us close, her calm mask of bravery betrayed by shaking hands. She seemed so mature and grown-up, but she was only in her early twenties.

BAM!

"Let me in, you bitch!" Mike roared.

BAM!

"I said, LET ME IN!"

BAM!

It felt like it took an eternity for his rage to subside, but when it finally did, he left us alone. We stayed locked there inside Fern's bedroom long after the slamming ended.

When Mom found out what happened she was forced to admit there was something wrong. But rather than call the cops or get a restraining order, she took Mike out for dinner one last time.

Bobbie and I both had to come.

For the final dinner with Mike, Mom took us to Mother Tucker's, an actual restaurant with separate booths, real menus and friendly waitresses. In retrospect, it seems bizarre that my sister and I had to share a table with the psycho who'd terrorized us only a few days earlier, but at the time it seemed completely normal, and I was far too preoccupied with our exotic surroundings to give the matter much thought.

While my mom calmly explained to Mike that he needed to move out, I spent the dinner engrossed in my milkshake and French fries. I was too young to appreciate the potential drama of this moment and didn't pay attention to what they said to each other. I do remember that the fries were excellent, and I slathered them in ketchup.

I suppose the dinner must have gone as well as could be expected. But that didn't mean the night went by without incident. Bobbie, just four and a bundle of hyperactive energy, quickly grew restless in our booth. It didn't take her long to stand up and start moving around. Mom and I didn't notice her, but Mike was already agitated, and his short fuse was burning.

"Sit down!" he roared as he reached across the table and slammed her tiny body against the glass-encased booth. She was too stunned to cry. Instead, she sat down as mom looked around to make sure no one was staring at us. That was the last time we ever saw Mike, but it wasn't the last time we lived with an aggressive and unstable man.

Red Ribbons

It's easy to remember the sunny days in Vancouver. They don't come often.

My first elementary school track and field event took place on one of those rare Vancouver days. The sun shone down upon us, blessing our little school with its radiance. Track and field day at Stoney Plain Elementary included running around pylons and carrying eggs with spoons while tying our legs together with a partner for the three-legged race. It wasn't exactly the sort of thing that put Carl Lewis on the Wheaties box, but to me it felt like the same thing.

I'd already been through a lot as a six-year-old. My parents divorced. We moved across the country from Miramichi, New Brunswick to Vancouver, British Columbia. Mom developed a lousy habit of bringing not-so-nice boyfriends home along with their drama and, all too often, violence.

Still, I wasn't thinking about any of those things the afternoon of my track meet. I was far too absorbed in the task at hand. I had one goal: COLLECT AS MANY RIBBONS AS I COULD.

Because they were handed out for first place finishers, I preferred the red ones with the gold print. I get that from my dad. Once he focuses on something, whether it's real estate or the stock market, he can't stop until he's mastered it.

I was the same way. Driven; some would say obsessed. That day, I wanted to win as many red ribbons as possible.

And I did.

It was amazing.

My best event was the sprint. I ran like a six-year-old version of Carl Lewis. I was faster than the boys, faster than the other girls and faster than anyone else—a trend I would continue for several years in track and for decades in business.

Thinking back to that afternoon makes me realize I've forgotten most of the details, such as the other kids' names and my teacher's name. But I'll always remember the joy I felt. I treasured those and many more earned ribbons into my teenage years, displaying them on the walls of my bedrooms. As the years went by, I needed joy more and more, but it took me many years to regain the feelings I had that day.

From One Loser to Another

As much as Bobbie and I loved them, Mom grew frustrated by the way she felt her sisters were interfering in her life. Not long after our dinner at Mother Tucker's, she moved us out of the house we shared with them.

Our new home was a duplex in Ganymede Close, a neighbourhood in the City of Burnaby. The caretaker of the duplex was a crude and sturdy guy named Steve. He had a young son about my age named Stevie.

Steve Sr. and mom quickly started dating.

Within a few months, we were all living together under one roof.

Unlike some of mom's previous boyfriends, Steve wanted to take the relationship to the next level. He even proposed to my mom, giving her an engagement ring he'd already used to propose to two other women. Claiming he was old-fashioned, he insisted my mom quit her job. Soon it became clear that this had less to do with traditional family values and more to do with his fear that any money she might earn would make her independent enough to leave him.

One night, as he and mom were in their bedroom with the door closed, his true colours came out.

Stevie, Bobbie and I were playing a game together. It was only a matter of time before our fun turned to tears. Something set Bobbie off, and she started howling loud enough to interrupt the grown-ups' secret bedroom activity. Steve reacted.

"You brat!" Steve shouted from behind the door. "How many times do I have to tell you?" he continued as he bolted out of the room, dressed only in a pair of ragged white jockey shorts. But it wasn't Bobbie he was after.

Stevie turned pale as he stiffened in front of us. He'd been through this before. "I'm sorry!" he apologized. "I didn't mean..." Steve didn't let Stevie continue, cutting him off with a hard spanking that knocked the boy off his feet.

Bobbie stopped crying, shocked by the suddenness of the violence. The two of us froze where we were standing, terrified that if we said or did anything, we'd receive the same response.

"I can't leave you alone for two seconds!" Steve went on, his face a purple blot of rage. "Get up!" he ordered.

Stevie hesitated, which only made his father angrier.

"I SAID, GET UP!"

Steve bent down and grabbed Stevie by his arm. To no avail, Stevie squirmed and struggled against his father's grasp. The more he struggled, the angrier his father became.

"Stop squirming!" Steve demanded as he landed another hard spank to Stevie's behind. And another.

Bobbie and I stayed still, barely allowing a breath. Steve ignored us, directing all his fury towards Stevie.

"Now," SPANK!

"Don't," SPANK!

"Make," SPANK!

"Me," SPANK!

"Come," SPANK!

"Out," SPANK!

"Here," SPANK!

"Again!" SPANK!

Stevie never cried. He fell to the ground shaking with terror when his father finally stopped. Steve turned around, went back to his bedroom, barging past mom who was standing in front of the doorway, and slammed the door behind him.

She never mentioned that night.

A few days later, we found ourselves in the same situation again— the three kids playing together while Steve and my mom played their own private game in the bedroom. We played "Mommy and Daddy" until Stevie grew bored, picked up the baby doll and swung it at my head as hard as he could. My head split open and produced a gushing stream of blood. As one might expect, chaos ensued. A couple of hours later, I found myself on the doctor's table as he closed the wound with a needle and surgical thread. I bawled through every step of the procedure.

Leaving Steve

Mom ignored Steve's abuse of his son, but she had enough of him when she came home one afternoon to find him forcing a bar of soap into Bobbie's mouth. This was the last straw. Mom waited until Steve went out and then called her friend Robbie to come to pick her and Bobbie up while I was at school.

Robbie arrived and Mom packed up a few essentials. In the middle of this task, they heard the sound of the door opening. Mom panicked and threw the small bag she was packing into her bedroom closet.

"Hey," Steve poked his head through the door, "is that Robbie's car parked outside?"

With her heart beating as fast as a hummingbird's wings, she managed to stay cool on the outside.

"Uh-huh," she answered him. "He's in the kitchen. He just came over to say, 'Hi.' What are you doing back so soon?"

"Got halfway there and realized I forgot my wallet in the jeans I wore yesterday," he told her. He walked over to a pile of clothes in the corner and lifted a pair of Levi's, retrieving his missing wallet.

Robbie appeared in their doorway.

"Hey Steve," he said calmly. "Thought you were at work."

"I should be. Forgot my wallet."

"That's no good," Robbie sympathized.

"Nope," Steve agreed as he walked out of the bedroom and out of the house.

Bouncing Around

Not having a lot of options, we found ourselves back in Port Coquitlam with my aunts. But after living there for a year, we returned to Burnaby and Ganymede Close. I was happy about this because I reunited with my friends who lived three houses down the street, Jamie and Jo-Jo.

The two brothers were adorable free spirits who zipped around the neighbourhood with the confidence of little emperors. I had a crush on Jo-Jo, but I also admired Jamie for his fearlessness. He would spend hours on his small bike, pretending he was the Fonz riding around on a motorcycle.

One day he even built a miniature version of the ramp Fonzie used to jump over 14 garbage cans in a classic episode of Happy Days. Fonzie ended up crashing into Arnold's fried chicken stand. Jamie broke his leg.

Still struggling on her own, my mom was working three jobs to keep our heads above water. After school each day a lovely woman named Ilene Hayter babysat Bobbie and me. Together we would sit and watch reruns of Gilligan's Island, which I thought was just about the funniest thing I had ever seen.

This routine was broken one week when Ilene had to go to the hospital for an operation, and mom found an alternative sitter for Bobbie and me. The replacement sitter brought her daughter, who was slightly older than me and insisted we play alone in my room. There she had me join her under the covers of my bed where she played a "game" she referred to as "Doctor."

Only when I eventually confronted the truth of my later sexual abuse did I see the girl's "game" for what it was. Knowing now what I do about child sexual abuse and how it affects its survivors, it's clear to me that the girl was a probable victim of abuse herself. Being abused didn't excuse her abusive behaviour.

Time for a Move

After two years in B.C., Mom and her sisters decided it was time to visit New Brunswick. It was during this visit that I met Mom's aunt and uncle, Irene and Fred. I immediately fell in love with them. When it came time to leave, I stood in the small foyer of their house and bawled my eyes out.

Six months following our return, Aunt Nancy showed up at our house looking like she'd seen a ghost. Never one to visit empty-handed, she arrived with a pair of adorable stuffed Monchhichi monkeys, which she gave to Bobbie and me. "Go play with these while I talk to your mommy," she told us with a slight quiver in her voice. We did as we were told but remained within earshot, listening to Aunt Nancy explain to our mom why she was upset.

Aunt Nancy had been dating a kind man named Andy, whom we all liked. What we didn't know was that in spite of his kindness, Andy did business with some evil men. Some of these men accused Andy of betraying them and wanted to punish his betrayal. Terrified by what this punishment might mean for everyone close to Andy, Aunt Nancy believed the entire family was in terrible danger. We had no choice but to move back to New Brunswick immediately.

If my mom was skeptical about her sister's fears, she didn't show it. She'd been thinking about returning to Miramichi ever since we got back from our earlier trip. She didn't mention it to anyone at the time, but she hit it off with a man named Pete during our visit to New Brunswick. Nancy's desperate desire to flee was the perfect opportunity to return, especially since Mom's terrified sister was more than willing to pay for our travel expenses.

I didn't know any of this at the time. All I knew was that my mom agreed to uproot us from what had become our home to go to a place where I had no friends. A place that was so small they might not even have red ribbons.

Jamie and Jo-Jo came by later to play, but all I could do was sit in the basement with Jo-Jo, crying and holding my brand new Monchhichi. The thought of never seeing them again overcame me.

Still, there was one bright spot. I'd only seen my dad twice since we moved out west, and I was excited by the thought of being with him again. Encouraged by the memory of my dad, I lifted my chin, wiped the tears from my eyes and focused on a future that was more uncertain than I knew.

CHAPTER 3

WELCOME TO MIRAMICHI

Your light was bright and new
But he didn't care
He took the heart of a little girl

— *Matthew West*

In Sight of a Predator

As we stepped outside the airport in St John, New Brunswick, I remembered the fun and good times we had when we visited a few months earlier. I looked forward to seeing my dad but wasn't thrilled when Aunt Nancy said we would be living with our grandmother, Helen. That meant living with her second husband, Wib. I never knew my real grandfather. He died when my mom was fifteen.

Ever since she was a teenager, my mom and aunts had issues with their stepfather. Wib's dislike for women was painfully obvious. Living in a house of teenage girls, he regularly referred to them as "a bunch of sluts," and never tried to hide his disdain.

My mom couldn't afford to be choosy, so the three of us moved into his already full home. He and my grandmother rented out the basement to three tenants. The upstairs of the house was for family—my grandmother, Wib, my mom, Bobbie, our cousin and myself.

The décor was filled with gaudy '70s knick-knacks, the type of stuff that would look kitschy if it were displayed today. In the early '80s, it was just tacky. Once again, Bobbie and I had no choice but to share a small room. Despite never having one of my own, I still resented the lack of privacy.

Spending Time With Dad

I would be remiss not to speak of my dad. He was absent during the early years, but as we settled into life in Miramichi, he played a more significant role in my upbringing. I saw him regularly, often spending the weekend at his house. My dad was a successful businessman, and from him I started to get a picture of my potential.

He wasn't counting quarters, dimes and pennies like my mom. I liked the idea of having more and eating out at restaurants. To this day, I love the feeling of eating out at a restaurant. I credit this to my dad. He never cooked for us, and on the rare occasion that he did, it was a comedy to see. The food itself was horrible.

My entrepreneurial bent comes from him. He worked in a bank as a young man before quitting to get into real estate. Against all the odds, he convinced the bank to give him a mortgage to buy an apartment building. He wasn't afraid to take a risk, and rewards came for his courage and hard work.

Dad is a bright man. In addition to being entrepreneurial, he had an appetite for knowledge. Books were his friends, and I was paid $10 for every book I read. He had his faults, too. His moods were up and down. Dad loved to talk and all too often we would sit in restaurants for three hours at a time as he went on and on with people. Sometimes we would go to the car and wait for him, hoping he would get the hint. Ironically, he somehow never seemed to have many close friends.

Dad always told me I was going to achieve great things. He saw something in me. And other than my track coach, who I'll mention later, he was the only one who treated me with optimism. I cherished my time with him. To this day, I credit much of my perseverance, success, and guts to his lessons and example. He showed me what I could be and what my way out would be.

Profile of a Monster

The hardest part of writing your life story is that you don't get to choose which characters play the most critical roles. If it were up to me, Wib would be a minor character at best. Mentioned a handful of times in one short chapter and then dismissed forever—a name you'd likely forget before the end of the page. Instead, he plays too significant of a role in my story.

This book wouldn't exist if not for him, but that's no compliment. He's the villain in these pages—the personification of everything I would later dedicate my life to fighting.

In describing Wib, I can't claim to be objective. I knew him as a monster. It's difficult to imagine him as anything else. His crimes were such that he does not deserve to be understood. In later years, I would attempt to do just that for my own mental and emotional freedom, but that doesn't mean he should be off the hook. He was a monster who should have been locked up.

One lesson I learned through the entire ordeal of my life is that people will delude themselves in any number of ways so as not to upset what they believe is a "perfect" family or community. Even after Wib's death in 2014, there was a glowing obituary written about him.

He was a deeply disturbed man to have committed the crimes he did. His crimes must never be forgotten, which is why I reiterate—Wib, and all perpetrators of child sexual abuse are monsters. There has never been proof that offenders are curable. And when a monster isn't curable, they need to be locked up.

One of the most important lessons people learn when they understand the realities of child sexual abuse, is that child molesters are not easily identifiable. Some have beards, and some are clean-shaven. Some have shifty suspicious eyes while others look stalwart and true. Much to our detriment, they can look and sound and dress like anyone.

Child sex offenders are priests, businessmen, teachers, coaches, accountants and any other profession. They are white, black, brown, green, purple or any colour.

Take Wib for example—he was a crossing guard at my elementary school and a respected member of the community. He attended church. He was tall, broad shouldered and slightly overweight. He always wore green or brown cotton pants and plaid shirts with a thick brown belt. Wib had a long face, huge brown eyes and glasses, and sported a comb-over. By the time we moved into his house, he had given up drinking, but still regularly popped pills.

He suffered from nightmares brought about by his days fighting in World War II. He was young in the war, as he lied about his age when he signed up to join the military. Wib was a mean, bitter and angry old man. He was unkind, which made the uncharacteristic generosity he occasionally showed to me very strange.

Though I felt the brunt of his impatience as much as anyone, he also singled me out for the kind attention he denied others. For no good reason, he'd often slip me some spare change and tell me I could go to Gumpy's, the local corner store, to spend however I wished. I inevitably used the money to splurge on penny candies.

It's clear now that this "kindness" was what's known as "grooming." Sexual predators use gifts, kindnesses or anything else to gain the trust of their future victims.

The End of Innocence

It was rare to find the house so empty. Only Bobbie, our babysitter Anne and I were there that New Year's Eve. Bobbie was already in bed asleep. Anne was on the telephone, talking to a friend, and it felt like I had the whole house to myself. It was New Year's Eve of 1981, and everyone was out celebrating—everyone except Wib. He was at an Alcoholics Anonymous meeting.

I remember feeling excited by the possibilities of an empty house because I would get to do whatever I wanted to do, so I played a game called Tip the Waiter while watching TV. Nothing good was on TV, and I was waiting for Dick Clark's New Year's Rockin' Eve. According to the commercial, it was going to be co-hosted by Luke Duke, which was more than reason enough for me to watch.

I heard someone come in the front door.

Anne, my babysitter, went to the door, and I heard talking. She came in the room, said goodbye, and that my grandfather would watch me. Wib came in shortly after and asked me who else was in the house.

"Bobbie," I said.

"Where is she?" he asked.

"She's asleep," I said.

"She wasn't allowed to stay up for New Year's?"

"She was, but she was too tired to stay awake."

"Uh-huh."

Thirty years later, I can interpret so many meanings in that, "Uh-huh," and I've spent days thinking about it. It never occurred to me at that time that I might not be the only person excited by an empty house.

I felt nervous. I'd never been alone in the house with Wib before. Sometimes he would give me money, but other times he was mean and grumpy, saying terrible things that frightened me. I found the friendly version of him creepier than the grumpy version because even at that age I could tell there was something false about it. It was a mask. He was hiding something.

"What game are you playing?" he asked.

I told him about Tip the Waiter. I played it before and liked it. Everyone received some fake money and some cardboard cutouts of food. In the middle of the game board was a cardboard waiter who held a serving tray over his head. You took turns putting food onto the tray, until the waiter's arm tipped over. Whoever made him drop the food had to give a dollar, and the last person to have any money left was the winner. I had a special knack for placing the food just right on the tray so it didn't tip over.

I sat on the floor in front of the couch, and I knew something odd was happening when Wib sat down beside me on the floor. He never sat on the floor.

"Do you want to play a game with me?" he asked.

I started thinking about how I was going to brag to everyone else that I'd beat him. We started the game, but as we played, it became clear that Wib's mind wasn't in the game. He was concerned about things that had nothing to do with the game.

Have you ever been talking with someone when they became distracted by a text message on their phone? They try to continue listening to the conversation and responding, but it's obvious their mind isn't present. That is how Wib was with Tip the Waiter, and from his distraction, I got a vague feeling of unease.

"Sit right here," he told me, indicating a spot next to him on the floor, in front of the couch.

I didn't want to. He smelled gross and musky. However, I could tell the difference between a kind suggestion and a direct command.

I moved closer to him.

We each took a few more turns, and every time he reached over to put food on the cardboard tray, he would slide closer to me until our legs were touching. I tried to ignore him and focus on the game. We only had a couple of pieces left, and the tray was clearly about to fall. It was his turn.

He picked up a piece at random and dropped it on top of the tray. The arm gave, and all of the food collapsed onto the board below.

"You have to tip the waiter!" I giggled happily. He only had two dollars left, and I still had all of mine.

He didn't tip the waiter.

Instead, he grabbed my hand.

He did it so quickly and suddenly that I didn't have a chance to protest. Before I could tell what was happening, he placed it onto the crotch of his pants and rubbed it back and forth.

I wanted to yank it away, but I was scared, and I didn't know what was happening.

"That's a good girl," he told me in his "nice" voice.

"Don't be frightened."

"You have to tip the waiter," I repeated—my voice shaking.

"What? Oh, that's right."

He let go of my hand and picked up a fake plastic dollar and stuck it to the waiter. I picked up the cardboard food pieces, divided them between us and lifted the waiter's arm back up. As I did this, Wib stood up, undid his belt and let his pants drop to the floor.

He then sat back down beside me and grabbed my hand again. This time he made me move my hands back and forth on his penis.

"Uh-huh," he smiled grotesquely. "That's it."

I was so confused. I knew this was wrong, but I didn't even know what it was or why he became so happy. Before I could start crying, he let go of my hand and grabbed the back of my head. He pushed down until my face and mouth were pressed down against his penis.

The horror went on for a while. I remember the uncomfortable feeling of gagging and shock.

"That's it," he started to say before being interrupted by the sound of the doorbell.

He swore with a mixture of both frustration and fear.

He let go of my head to go to the door, and I ran to my bedroom while he bent over to pick up his pants. Bobbie was still sleeping soundly and didn't rouse as I scrambled into the bed we shared, terrified about what might happen next. Facing her nose-to-nose, I clamped my arms around her and squeezed. She locked my head in her arms, and I couldn't move.

I tried to calm myself, hoping and praying he'd leave me alone if he thought I was asleep. My heart fluttered and boomed as I pressed my ear against the pillow.

Time passed.

I heard the front door close and the sound of footsteps approaching our bedroom. Our door clicked open, and Wib came into the room, smelling his gross, musky smell as he stood above me.

He breathed heavily.

I wanted to open my eyes to see what was happening, but I was terrified he would realize I wasn't asleep and make me go back to the living room where I couldn't escape. I didn't move an inch. I can only guess what mental calculations he was making at that moment, weighing risks and the odds of another interruption to his vile "game." After an eternity of him standing over the bed, he left the bedroom, taking his gross smell with him.

I was safe for the rest of that night, but the abuse had just begun. Wib continued like this for the next two years, cornering me whenever he could, making me do things I didn't want to do. I could recount all of the instances of abuse here in these pages, but in truth, I don't want the abuse to be the focal point of this book.

The incident I described above was horrific, but others were far worse.

It happened whenever Wib found me alone—in the house, in the car, in the bathtub and on the beach.

His abuse involved objects, forced touching, penetration and forced fellatio.

It was horrible.

I endured the violence dozens of times over two years, living in fear of my abuser.

The trauma brought me within an inch of slicing my wrists. Suicide seemed like a preferred option to end the pain.

There are many phases of survival for victims of sexual abuse. The first is to survive the abuse itself.

CHAPTER 4

A SURVIVOR IS BORN

"I think it's the human spirit inside of all of us that has an enormous capacity to survive."
— *Amanda Lindhout*

Memories of St. Andrews School

It doesn't take much thought to understand why a pedophile or a child molester might volunteer for jobs that would put them near young children. In this horrible business of pedophilia or child molesting, the only reliable pattern is that most abusers manipulate their way into a position of trust long before the abuse begins.

Wib spent time each day leading my fellow students at St. Andrews Elementary across the street as our official crossing guard. He treated the role like you'd expect of a former soldier with severe control issues, reigning over the crosswalk like a tyrant, treating the kids and drivers with equal severity as he halted their progress with his sign.

For me, this meant I couldn't escape him, even at school, even on the way to school, as I had to ride in the car with him to school every morning. These rides were always tense and silent.

When he abused me in the car I would go to another place in my mind by playing with the windows. Roll them up. Roll them down. I would think about what I would do the next day. Change the radio stations. Play with the buttons. Anything but what was just about to happen. It was very clear when it was about to go down.

He would take me to the beach. There lots of areas in Miramichi to pull off the road onto a beach.

I couldn't fight him.

Bobbie remembers that he came into our room and took me away and she knew it wasn't right. The devastation in a family goes beyond the abused. Bobbie suffers from false guilt. "I should have done something."

But there was nothing she could have done.

I experienced blackouts. I don't remember all of my abuse. There are lapses in time periods of my childhood.

Everything was about trying to avoid him. Trying to be safe. In the end there was no getting away from him.

In my heart, I knew what he was doing was wrong. Wib never showed any shame or remorse about it. Still, he guarded the secrecy of the situation intensely, and he added a new dimension of fear to my life one morning when he broke the customary silence.

"Do you love your mom and your sister?" he asked me.

"Uh-huh," I answered hesitantly, surprised by the question.

"Wouldn't it be terrible if something bad happened to them?"

"Uh-huh."

"Well, something bad is going to happen to them."

"Why?" I asked him, terrified.

"I'm going to kill them."

I tried to protest, but the thought of him murdering my family was too much, and I burst into tears instead.

"You didn't let me finish," he continued. "What I was going to say was that I'm going to kill them, unless."

"Unless what?" I managed to burble out through my tears.

"Unless you promise not to tell anyone about the," he struggled to find the right word, "games we sometimes play."

"I won't tell," I pleaded with him. "I promise. Please don't hurt them. I promise I promise, I promise, I promise, I promise."

"Okay, that's enough. I believe you. Now clean up your face. I don't want you looking like a mess when you get out of the car."

I did as I was told. I had to, now that I knew my mom and sister's lives depended on it.

My time at St. Andrews was terrifying due to Wib's constant presence, but I have a couple of great memories from there. At the top of the list is the time I learned that I have what it takes to be a competitive runner. It happened on the playground one day when a boy with a reputation for speed challenged me to a race. His name was David, and when I beat him in a sprint between soccer goalposts, my reputation for running was born.

More importantly, it reminded me of the red ribbons and the exceptional talent in myself. Self-belief is rare in an abuse survivor, but when I saw my power as a runner, I grabbed at it and held on with everything I had. After that race with David, I vowed to be the fastest.

An Eventual Reprieve

The pattern of abuse went on for about two years—me surviving the abuse, mom not knowing what was happening, and him cornering me whenever he could.

Mom continued her relationship with Pete, her schoolteacher boyfriend, whom she met on that first trip back to Miramichi. They had gotten closer during those two years. It meant she was gone more often, which left more time for Wib to do what he wanted. In addition to developing a relationship with Pete, Mom was also working on getting us into a home of our own. Eventually, we moved into a trailer park and a new school, St. Michaels Elementary.

The trailer park was like something out of a movie—full of losers. People drank and smoked pot on the front steps of their trailers. Children roamed the neighbourhood.

Bobbie and I shared a bedroom. It was so small that when I laid in my little bunk bed, my feet would touch the wall. We couldn't even fit a dresser in the room. It was 600 square feet, and for some reason, I took the game, Tip the Waiter with me.

Strangest of all, there were two little girls, Lauren and Julie, living in another trailer. They were Wib's niece's daughters. We played in their backyard playhouse. Years later I learned Wib had also sexually abused them.

As bizarre as it sounds, our situation paints an accurate picture of child sexual abuse. Two moms, doing their best, but only able to afford the cold comfort of a cheap little trailer in a scummy part of town. Their daughters both abused by the same man who lived with impunity in a comfortable home.

Other than the memory of the shabbiness of the trailer park and the years-later revelation that my little playmates were fellow survivors, there wasn't too much memorable about our stint in the trailer park. We lived there for a short time before moving in with mom's schoolteacher boyfriend and his twin daughters, Tasha and Cassandra. They stayed with us on weekends at our new place in another neighbourhood called Douglasfield.

I had mixed emotions about this. I didn't like Pete from the day he rang the doorbell at my grandparents' house to take Mom on a date. Pete and Mom spent quite a bit of their time drinking—both when he would visit us in the trailer park and when we all lived together in Douglasfield. I didn't like that, but what I didn't like even more was having Pete control my life. He wanted to be in control of everything I did, and it didn't sit well with me.

Pete was the kind of man that wouldn't let you go to the local Field's store without a coupon for toilet paper. Worse were the drinking episodes. There were several physical altercations between Pete and my mom while they were both drunk. He put us down verbally. We could never measure up to his daughters in his eyes. They were great. They were going to be successful and happy. Bobbie and I would always be losers in his eyes.

I wanted to move out of his house and live with my dad. It wasn't meant to be, so I had to learn to get along. I never gave in, though. Pete and I may not have gotten along, but on the positive side, Tasha and Cassandra were my best friends while we lived together. I adored them because they were so loving and kind, the best part of the relationship between Mom and Pete.

And at least we were no longer living with Wib. I'd take Pete and his craziness any day over the hell of living with Wib.

Not Fitting In

In Vancouver, I was a popular outgoing kid at school, but that all changed in Miramichi. In a small town, where everyone knew each other, the "new kid" meant having to go through a lengthy trial period before the other kids decided you were worth accepting into their social circle. My antisocial behaviour and irregular bathing habits turned me into an elementary school pariah.

Things didn't change much when I moved to St. Michaels School. I no longer had the stigma of riding to school with Wib but I exhibited enough weird behaviour to remain mostly on the outside. However, I wasn't completely alone at St. Michaels.

I had one friend, a girl in my class named Joan. She was a lot like me. Quiet, secretive, unclean, and strange in a way the other kids couldn't figure out. We found ourselves drawn to each other and formed our social circle of two.

When you're an outcast, recess and lunch are often the worst parts of the day. Imagine being forced to attend a party where you know no one likes you. The best you can hope for is to be left alone and allowed to stand by yourself in the corner of the room. Now imagine doing this three times a day, five days a week.

Childhood can be a terrifying time, even for kids who don't have to worry about what their step-grandfather is going to do to them when they get home. Whether it's sexual abuse, physical abuse, ostracism, bullying or neglect, it's impressive that so many of us even make it to our teens. Kids are so strong. They have to be.

Joan and I avoided the recess/lunch trap the only way we knew how. We hid by ducking into a mechanical room downstairs. It was dark but safe. Besides, both of us were used to hiding in weird spaces. We talked with imaginary friends. I liked to think of mine as spirits who followed me wherever I went.

It wasn't a coincidence that Joan and I were so much alike. She had an uncle living with her family who snuck into her bedroom at night and insisted on "playing games." Joan hated those games, but she didn't tell her parents about them because her uncle promised to hurt them badly if she did.

But her uncle had left a loophole. He never told her she couldn't tell a friend about the "games," so she told me. Caught up in the moment I told her about Wib. When given a chance, the words flew out of my mouth. I so desperately needed to tell someone that they came out in a torrent, even though Wib hadn't left me any loopholes.

When I finished, I burst into tears. Not because I'd finally said the words out loud, but because I was sure that Wib would find out I told someone and make good on his threat to kill Mom and Bobbie. I knew Joan wouldn't tell anyone. Still, I thought he would find out somehow, that perhaps we'd be at a family gathering and my confession to Joan would show up on my face, as big and visible as a billboard.

But he didn't find out. I wish I could say that learning this gave me the bravery I needed to tell the people who could do something to stop him, but that's not how this story goes.

Nor is it how most abuse stories go. Perhaps the saddest fact of child sexual abuse is that even if a child finds the courage to tell, it doesn't mean they'll find someone willing to listen.

Moving On

When my mom told us she was getting married to Pete, it didn't come as much of a surprise. Still, I wasn't happy about it. Pete appeared to be different from the usual jerks mom dated. He had a stable job as a teacher, but he also had weird energy I couldn't put my finger on. Being a teacher, he was comfortable with kids, but I never got the sense that he liked me. Bobbie and I were just part of the deal.

The house in Douglasfield had several outbuildings, which we used for hide-and-seek. We spent a lot of time playing in the spacious yard, and in continuing with my school habit, I spent a lot of time talking to my imaginary friends. I thought the house was haunted. I was always spooked there. Two different people died on the property, and strange things happened like the toilet flushing randomly when nobody was in the bathroom.

I never slept soundly in that house, but my mom loved Douglasfield. She lived there with her family when she was a kid. It was where they lived when her dad died. After a couple of years in Douglasfield, we moved again, this time to a beautiful house on Cedar Street. It was a brown and white Tudor style home in a good neighbourhood. We were now back across town in Chatham, yet we continued to go to St. Michaels Elementary, which meant a long bus ride to school.

Bobbie and I continued to share a bedroom. Tasha and Cassandra had their bedroom, which they used on weekends when they stayed with us. I still hated baths, and my mom always had to fight to get me to take one. I survived bath time by talking to my imaginary friends.

Nightmares about the abuse plagued my sleep, and I was afraid of what Wib would do to me. Not living with him meant it was easier to avoid him, but he was still my grandfather, and there were still plenty of occasions to be in his company.

My family went to church every Sunday. Wib was always there. We had plenty of family gatherings, and as much as he seemed to despise everyone, he still showed up. Worst of all was the fear. Once violated, it's nearly impossible for a child to feel safe. I suspected everyone, sticking only to the select few people I trusted. I was very much stuck in survival mode in the years immediately after the abuse.

Unbeknownst to me, the worst was yet to come.

CHAPTER 5

THE TRUTH COMES OUT, AND NO ONE CARES

"You are far more than your worst day, your worst experience, your worst season. You are more than the darkest sorrow you've endured. Your name is not Helpless. Not only are you capable, you have full permission to move forward in strength and health."

— *Jen Hatmaker*

A Chance to Tell the Truth

Wib started sexually abusing me when I was eight years old, and he didn't stop until I moved out two years later. I kept quiet about the abuse, believing he still had power over me. I lived in constant fear.

One evening when I was twelve, my mom came to me with a shocking revelation of her own rape experience. She had a few drinks that night and needed to get it off her chest. Looking back, I know it was an attempt to protect me from the very thing that had already happened. Even in her worst nightmares, she couldn't have imagined that it had already happened to me.

It happened to Mom when she was fourteen. She was walking home along the railroad tracks when an older boy approached her. She resisted, but he overpowered her and raped her right there on the railroad tracks. Mom got home and hid her bloody clothes. Grandma found them, but she either ignored the truth, or my mom made up a plausible story because nothing ever came of it.

Years later, when I found the courage to reflect truly, it horrified me that my abuse was just another step in a multi-generational pattern. It happened to my mom, it happened to me and it happened to other members of my family.

With my mom's disclosure of her rape out in the open, I felt safe to tell her about Wib's abuse. I probably should have waited until another time because, in her emotional and intoxicated state, she wasn't prepared to hear what I had to say.

"Mom?" I tested the waters, seeing if she was prepared to listen to me.

"Yes, sweetie?"

I hesitated, realizing I didn't have the words to say what I was about to say.

She picked up on the gravity of my hesitation. "What is it, Glori?"

"You know what?" I tried it again.

"What?"

"The same thing happened to me."

"What?"

"At Grandma's."

"What happened?" She was alarmed.

"It was...Wib."

Mom froze. "What about Wib?"

"Sometimes, he would...do...bad things. He made me do bad things."

"What sorts of things?"

"He...touched me."

"What?"

"And made me touch him."

The colour drained out of her face.

"He touched you."

I nodded.

"Where?"

I showed her.

She screamed and what she did next startled and scared me as I'd never seen her so angry. I didn't know she was even capable of being that angry. She reached into the kitchen drawer and grabbed a butcher knife. I held my breath, waiting for Pete to come in after hearing Mom scream. Then I remembered he was out doing some errand. My mom was hysterical, and I didn't know what to do.

"I'll kill him!" she screamed. "I'll cut his balls off and let him bleed to death!"

"Mom," I started to cry. "You're scaring me."

"That pervert!" she explained. "That pervert raped you."

I was terrified that she was going to run out of the house and do something stupid. I knew that if she tried to confront Wib, someone would get hurt. She might even end up in jail for murdering him.

"Calm down, mom," I pleaded with her. "Please calm down."

Upon hearing my words, all the fight in her instantly drained out of her body, and she slid to the kitchen floor, letting go of the knife and sobbing.

"It's okay, Mom," I ran over to her and held her. I knew it wasn't, but it was the only thing I could think of to say.

"How many times?" she pleaded when she stopped crying long enough to get the words out. "How many times did he touch you?"

"I don't know," I answered honestly, "a lot."

"Why didn't you say anything?"

"He told me he would kill you. And Bobbie."

"He did what?"

"Please don't tell him I told you," I begged her.

"He isn't going to hurt us, Glori," she promised as she hugged me back. "He isn't going to hurt anyone ever again. I'll make sure of that."

At that moment, we both believed it. We thought the truth was all we needed. Once we set it free, everything would be different.

We were so naïve.

Professional "Help"

It had been hard enough telling my mother, but a couple of days later she wanted me to tell a stranger with social services. I was hesitant, but I reluctantly agreed because of the promise of a Mc-Donald's visit afterward. We still didn't have much money, so a rare visit to McDonald's was enough to get me to do something very uncomfortable.

When we stepped inside the waiting room, I could tell it was a sad place. It was mostly adults, and none of them looked happy to be there. Behind a closed door somewhere we could hear a man shouting. "I told you!" he kept insisting over and over again. "The boy fell down the stairs!"

I looked up at my mom to see how she felt about where we were.

"We'll be out of here soon, Glori," she assured me, but I could tell she was just as scared as me.

Our appointment was for 9:45 a.m., but we had to sit in the waiting room until 11:00 am. I impatiently flipped through a tattered copy of *Highlights for Children*, which I'm sure was older than me. The whole office smelled terrible.

Finally, the woman we were supposed to see was ready for us. I got up to go with my mom, but the woman stopped me.

"I have to speak to your mother first," she told me. "Wait here until I call you in."

I wanted to ask her what the magic words were, but I knew that adults never liked it when you pointed out their lack of manners. Just looking at her told me that she wasn't someone I wanted to talk to. She was old, unhappy, and her hair was in a scruffy bun on top of her head. If Bobbie had been there, she would have insisted the woman was a witch, but I knew better. She just looked like a witch.

My eyes took in my surroundings, and my mom noticed the unease I felt at being alone. "Don't worry," she said. "It won't be long, and I'll just be a few feet away."

I nodded glumly and sat back down on the uncomfortable chair. I felt a sudden urge to burst into tears, but I fought against it with everything I could. My mom and the woman walked into the office and closed the door behind them. I picked up the tattered magazine and reread "Goofus and Gallant" from the *Highlights for Children*.

Goofus was being rude to his grandparents, while Gallant was polite and kind to his. I wondered if maybe Goofus had a reason for acting the way he did, but I still admired Gallant for doing the right thing.

Eventually, the door opened, and my mom and the woman walked out. "Come with me, Glori," said the woman. "We're going to have a chat."

We followed the woman into her small office and watched as she sat down behind her desk. Up close, she looked even scarier.

"Sit down, Glori," she told me, indicating the chair in front of her desk. Again she seemed unable to say "please." Once I was sitting, she started talking. "Your mother says something happened to you. Is that right?"

"Uh-huh," I nodded.

"Can you tell me about it?"

I looked at my mom and started to squirm.

"I want to hear the story in your words. I don't want your mom helping you. Do you understand?"

I didn't, but I nodded as though I did.

"So tell me what happened. Why are you here?"

"Wib," I answered her.

"Is he your grandfather?"

I shook my head.

"He isn't?"

"He's my step-grandfather," I corrected her.

"I see. What about your step-grandfather?"

"He...."

"Yes?"

"He touched me...and made me touch him."

"How did he touch you? I need you to be specific."

"He touched...my privates." My voice was barely above a whisper.

"Where? Can you show me?"

I pointed.

"And you said he made you touch him?"

"Yeah."

"Where?"

I pointed once again.

"How many times did he do this?"

"A lot."

"How much is a lot? Everyday? Once a week? A couple of times a month?"

"I don't know," I told her. "It happened a lot."

"Is it still happening?"

"No."

"Why not?"

"Because we moved."

"How long has it been since you moved?"

"About a year. Maybe more."

"When did you tell your mother?"

"Two days ago."

"Why didn't you tell her a year ago? Back when it was still happening?"

"I was scared."

"Why were you scared?"

"He said he'd kill my mom and my sister if I told."

"And you believed him."

"Uh-huh," I nodded.

"Did he do anything to make you think he'd kill your mom and sister?"

"He told me."

"Besides telling you."

"No."

"Your mother told me she's recently gotten remarried."

"Uh-huh. To Pete."

"Do you like Pete?"

"He's okay."

"Do you feel like you get less attention now that you're living with Pete?"

"I don't know."

"I'm sure you do know."

The interrogation went on for another ten minutes before the woman told me to go back to the waiting room. Then she and my mom spent another five minutes talking in her office.

When my mom walked out of the office alone she leaned in to me as we were leaving and quietly said, "I believe you, Glori, and I love you."

Then we went to McDonald's.

The Bad News

A few days passed. I was sitting in front of the TV, watching a game show, when the phone rang. I heard my mom pick it up in the kitchen. I could tell by the way she answered that it was the scary lady from social services.

"We won't be pursuing charges against Wib," was the first thing mom heard.

"Why not?" she asked angrily.

"I interviewed him personally yesterday," the woman told her. "He denied ever doing anything inappropriate with your daughter, and I believe him."

"But she told you what happened!"

"Children like Glori are prone to exaggeration."

"What do you mean, 'children like Glori'?"

"From a broken home, with a new stepfather. We see it all the time. She's just looking for attention."

"So, you're just going to take his word over hers?"

"I discussed the matter with Wib very thoroughly. He struck me as a very reasonable and agreeable man and certainly not someone who seeks sexual gratification from children. He's a very nice man and loves kids. He's a crosswalk guard."

"I can't believe this. He raped my daughter!"

"That's a serious accusation Ma'am, the kind that can ruin a man's life. We need more to go on than just the word of a twelve-year-old girl."

"So, you're not going to do anything?"

"There's nothing left to do."

"But what about the other children who are around him? My niece, my cousin and the kids at the school?"

"They're perfectly safe. I can assure you of that."

My step-grandfather was never investigated.

The Aftermath

I ran to the room I shared with Bobbie and cried, not because the woman didn't believe me. I cried because she had talked to Wib about the abuse. Now he knew I told, and I didn't know what he would do about it.

A thousand nightmare scenarios ran through my head. I saw him breaking into the house at night with an axe in his hand. I pictured him waiting outside the house in the morning with a shotgun. I imagined him sneaking in while we were out and poisoning our food.

"Why did you tell? Why did you tell? Why did you tell?" I kept repeating to myself over and over. Telling my mom had backfired, and it seemed like a colossal mistake. I thought this was the worst possible situation and that it couldn't get any worse, but it did.

Infuriated by the social worker's refusal to do anything about Wib's abuse, my mom decided to seek her manner of justice by calling a family meeting to discuss the situation. Along with my mom, Pete, myself and the rest of my Miramichi aunts and uncles were there—Elsie, Fern, and Dan, Cam and Louise.

My mom wanted to resolve my situation and protect the other children, including my cousin. She was close to my age and still lived with my grandmother and Wib. The meeting was a total disaster. That one night drove a permanent wedge in my family that endures to this very day, and I still bare the brunt of the blame.

My mom could never have expected that they would turn on me as they did. With the revelation of his abuse, they branded me a liar, a slut and a whore. Mom and Pete were the only ones who defended me. To the rest of them, I instantly became the troublemaking girl who refused to shut up and wanted to destroy the family.

I was sitting in the kitchen with everyone, but soon the names and accusations were too much. My Aunt Fern led me away from the kitchen into the living room. This time I took little comfort in her presence.

After a few moments in the living room, I ran to my bedroom and curled into the fetal position, still listening to the sounds of my family fighting over my inconvenient and uncomfortable truth. I sobbed myself to sleep.

The fighting went on for hours. The main topic of the argument was not how to help me, but whether or not to tell my grandmother, deemed too weak to handle the situation. Even though she was only in her fifties, most of the family thought she would certainly die of a heart attack at the thought of the accusations flying in the direction of her Wib. There was very little concern granted to the twelve-year-old girl who'd already been traumatized by something that no child should ever have to go through. My uncle Cam and his wife Louise were the angriest. They didn't want anyone to know what had happened.

In spite of all the reasons for my family to break up, they always stuck together. They were a stick-it-out type of family, no matter what. While that kind of loyalty is admirable, it comes with obvious drawbacks. For example, what if the biggest threat to family unity is from within rather than from without? That was the case with our family. Cam and Louise especially didn't want anyone else to ever learn the truth of our messed up little clan, and they were willing to silence me to protect it.

I'd learn in later years that my family would 'like' me as long as I was silent. But the silence forced upon me was a horrible burden to bear. It nearly tore me apart, and I didn't start healing until I started speaking up. The family meeting taught me one thing. If I was going to survive the rest of my life with anything resembling a family, I'd better keep my mouth shut.

The horror of Wib's abuse was compounded tenfold by my silencing at the hands of our family. A boy or girl can be hurt and abused, but the day he or she is told they don't deserve to voice the hurt, or be believed, is the day their spirit is crushed.

Too scared and frightened to run away for real, I did the only thing I could. I ran away inside my mind. I closed my eyes and imagined a world where none of this had happened. Where I had never left Vancouver, where my real grandfather never died, and where my grandmother never met or married Wib. I imagined a world where my family and the social services lady believed what I told them.

The little world inside my head didn't match the external reality, though. It wasn't until the night of the family meeting that I started experiencing extreme anxiety and panic attacks, the disorders that would haunt me over the next decades.

A Widespread Charade

The family meeting resolved only one thing—my grandmother could not be told about any of this. Outwardly, it was to protect her health, but the truth was that it swept Wib's abuse under the rug. Everyone wanted to pretend like it never happened.

My grandmother was a short woman with big black glasses. She grew up in poverty and had a submissiveness to Wib and his whims that characterizes so many women living in poverty. Her first husband died when my mom was fifteen. He dropped dead of a heart attack. Like many women of her generation, she went in search of a new man to take care of her. She had no way to earn money and take care of her family financially.

Before meeting Wib my grandmother and her kids were dependent on the kindness of fellow community members. People would drop off bags of food at their door to help them keep body and soul together. She knew struggle and despair as well as anyone.

My grandmother was a loving and warm woman, always making things with her capable hands and compassionately involved in the community. I always wondered why she was married to Wib—a man who was a jerk even to those he wasn't sexually abusing.

I now know the answer. Grandma was dependent on him financially. She didn't know how to take care of herself. Maybe it was this dependence and helplessness that made the rest of the family want to protect her so much. She had already "been through so much," and nobody wanted to put more of a burden on her.

It fell to me to take the brunt of the burden, so we all pretended. At times, even my mom wasn't immune to this. She wanted the best for me, but becoming an outcast with her family was too much. Things returned to "normal."

I frequently found myself back in Wib's house and was forced to pretend like nothing was wrong. In front of everyone, he would call me over and tell me to sit on his lap. In a healthy family, this would be nothing more than an affectionate gesture from a loving grandfather, but he wasn't a loving grandfather, and we weren't a healthy family. Knowing I was already under the microscope and that my survival depended upon conforming, I did as I was told.

I can't begin to explain how wrong and creepy it felt to sit on Wib's lap. At church and weddings, I was forced to sit beside him, too.

All I wanted was for someone to love me, and I began praying for God to protect me and for ONE person to love me wholly.

I once heard about a tradition in pagan societies where they would select a girl to sacrifice to the gods during times of trouble, with the hope that their offering would bring better times. In the name of keeping the peace, my family chose to sacrifice me.

The difference was that those other girls were honoured and revered for giving up their lives. I was resented and dismissed.

CHAPTER 6

LITTLE WARRIOR

"Vulnerability sounds like truth and feels like courage. Truth and courage aren't always comfortable, but they're never weakness."

— *Brené Brown*

Becoming a Little Warrior

It was because of the high regard I held for my dad that I didn't want to tell him about the abuse I suffered. My model for sharing my truth wasn't too good. Most everyone I loved had turned on me once I came clean with the facts, and I wasn't about to let that happen with my dad. I kept him in the dark because I wanted to stay daddy's little girl. I needn't have worried. He always supported me, but I didn't know that at the time.

It was at my dad's house where I made a transformation that would define the rest of my life. The change helped me in many ways, but it also had its drawbacks.

I became a warrior.

I knew my family hated me. Most of the time, I felt utterly alone in the world. Though they would never say so, I could tell that even those who believed me resented the fact that I didn't keep my misery to myself. Still, their resentment was preferable to the outright hatred I received from the others who believed I'd made the whole story up out of some malicious attempt to destroy Wib's life.

But his life wasn't destroyed. The social worker thought of him as a great guy. He still worked as a crossing guard at the school.

He was still married to my grandmother. She would never leave him no matter the accusations against him. They hated me for the trouble they felt I caused.

Now I was the one alone in my dad's bathroom, holding a pathetic little razor over my wrist, ready to put a permanent end to a life that hadn't begun. The blade didn't look like something that could end a life. Still, I heard it worked.

Kids at school were disturbingly knowledgeable about the details of how one might commit suicide.

Hanging was definitely out of the question. "People think it's quick," I remember one boy saying, "but only if it's done by a professional. They know how to place the knot perfectly so it'll snap your neck immediately. If people do it themselves, they put the knot in the wrong place and dangle there for minutes, slowly strangling to death. It takes a lot longer than people think."

I liked the idea of taking pills—of going to sleep and never waking up. But the only pills in my dad's medicine cabinet were an expired bottle of aspirin, and I knew the four that remained wouldn't be enough to get the job done.

Our small town didn't have any skyscrapers to jump off. I had no access to a car. Putting a plastic bag over my head didn't seem any different from hanging. Guns scared me.

That just left slitting my wrists.

I hated the sight of blood, but I considered this a bonus. It might cause me to faint and spare me the minutes it took for me to bleed to death. But I had no idea where the blade was supposed to go. Where was the magic spot that would end everything?

Figuring out how to do it was difficult. I hated doing it, but I didn't want to feel anymore. I sat there on my dad's bathroom floor, holding the blade over my wrist, waiting for the courage to slash. Closing my eyes, I held my breath. Something had to change. I couldn't go on like this anymore.

With my eyes still closed, I began to breathe again. I lay down on my back and imagined that I was somewhere else—that I was someone else.

This other person was taller than me. Older. Stronger. She had the build of an athlete. She was a runner with powerful and muscular legs. She leaped over hurdles with grace and power. She didn't acknowledge the hatred and resentment surrounding her. She used it only as fuel to propel her past the others, her outstretched chest always the first to break the tape crossing the finish line.

This other version of me didn't wait for anyone's approval. She won it herself. I knew this person. I discovered her in the hand where I still gripped the razor blade.

I opened my eyes and dropped the razor. I sat up on my knees and clasped my hands together and began to pray. "Please, God," I whispered, "please give me strength." I waited for a sign, but nothing came. There was only silence and my fierce determination to live. It took me a second to realize I no longer wanted to kill myself. Something had changed inside me.

It was at that moment that Little Glori went away. I was no longer a kid.

I could no longer accept the idea of giving up, especially when it meant letting those who had driven me to this point off the hook. I didn't have the language for it at that time, but that was the day I became a Warrior.

CHAPTER 7

BEE STINGS AND BAD SITUATIONS

"The young always have the same problem—how to rebel and conform at the same time."

— *Quentin Crisp*

They Fake, I Suffer

Junior high school years are often the worst in life. Grades seven through nine are the years when girls start making the physical transition towards becoming women, and boys begin seriously noticing the development the girls are making.

It's the time when the bullying escalates from name-calling and playground shoving into emotional terrorism. For most folks, this is when the person they end up becoming later in life truly starts to develop—where the molded clay begins to harden. However, I wasn't most people.

By grade eight, I'd already experienced a lifetime's worth of drama and dysfunction. My parents were divorced, and my mom had remarried. I'd moved across the country and witnessed the violent rampages of the men in my mother's life. We had returned to Miramichi under threat of gangland execution. I was forced to live in the same house as a child molester who repeatedly abused me. By age thirteen, when I finally found the courage to tell my story of sexual abuse, I'd been called a slut and liar by my extended family. Social services did mostly the same thing. I had stood at the brink of suicide, only to pull myself up out of the darkness.

Compared to that, junior high school was a walk in the park. I was a battle-scarred survivor. Nothing could break me down after what I'd experienced. Or so I thought, until one warm spring day at lunchtime.

The sun was shining bright, and there wasn't a cloud in sight. Bobbie and I were sitting on a step in front of my house. It was the first time my mom had ever left us without adult supervision, as she attended a wedding. We were basking in the sunshine when Bobbie suddenly shouted, "Bee!" Unfortunately, it settled on me, and I screamed with pain as it plunged its stinger into me.

Never having been stung, the shock scared me, but I had also heard about people having adverse allergic reactions to bee stings. I'd already been having panic attacks for a few years by this time, and I was having one now. It happened long before cell phones were an everyday use, so reaching my mom was futile. Bobbie called my grandmother, who told me to take two aspirins, but by now, my body was starting to swell up, and I was having difficulty breathing.

Bobbie told our grandmother what was happening, and she responded, "Wib is on his way." Great. I didn't need this.

By now, I was getting quite scared of what might happen, so I had no choice but to get in the car with him and go to the hospital. He drove me directly to the hospital, and on top of the swelling and difficulty breathing, I was also in an extreme state of fear sitting beside him in the car.

When my mom and Pete showed up at the hospital sometime later, I was on an IV, and the nurse told them I'd gone into anaphylactic shock. I'm lucky I got to the hospital within twenty minutes, or I might very well have died.

The whole episode looked like a typical medical situation—if I were a normal kid with a typical family. But in so many ways, it was symbolic of my life and the state of my psyche. A bee sting is a small thing for most people. It hurts for a moment and then goes away, but for those of us with bee venom allergies, that little thing can be deadly. It's much the same with trauma. For those that carry it, seemingly small things can set us off.

Wib showing up was too symbolic for comfort. In terms of physical proximity, I was no longer living with him. But in the back of my mind I wasn't safe from him. I always felt that he could show up and harm me at any moment. My fear was confirmed at a moment of great vulnerability.

Finally, there was my family's casual disregard for the state of my fragile psyche. The fact that my grandmother would send Wib to pick me up at all, never mind during a scary medical emergency, speaks volumes to how aware or how much my family cared for my mental well-being after the abuse.

Making the Best of a Bad Situation

It would be so easy for me to blame my mom for not slaying the ogre of my nightmares. It would have been nice if she could have wiped away the pain, like God. But she was human just like me, and didn't have the answers for the cruelty of the painful silence. She did the best with what she had. We all do.

My business instincts came from my dad. My care and love came from my mom. She had a huge heart, but just like my grandmother, she was very submissive.

Dad and mom were terrible worriers, too. My anxiety issues bear a striking resemblance to the anxiety they felt.

My mom chose crazy boyfriends. Pete was better, but even he, and, let's be honest, my dad (to an extent), represented the same pattern. They were overbearing and controlling men who liked to be in charge. Mom didn't have a backbone, and she never recovered emotionally from her own dad's death. But she cared deeply for me, and she did the best she could, given the tools she had.

It was mom's love for me that convinced her to accept the family's idea of me undergoing hypnosis to get to the truth of the matter. My mom learned that it was impossible for a person to lie under hypnosis, and she believed that once Wib and I were both hypnotized, it would prove I was telling the truth. She still naively believed that once the truth was out that the family would all support me.

The others wanted their definitive proof, so they thought it was a good idea, too. I wasn't convinced. As usual, my life was the battleground. Worse, I was still terrified of Wib and believed that if anybody had the power to resist hypnosis, it was him.

Going Under

"I want you to close your eyes. Can you do that for me, Glori?" said the hypnotist.

"I guess."

The small office was located in an old house a couple of hours away from ours. The room was designed to be as relaxing as possible, which seemed appropriate, yet it wasn't quite right. The hypnotist was an older lady with unruly white hair. The impression she left me with was that of a nun.

In spite of her best efforts to make the atmosphere right, the whole scenario was just creepy. It was like something out of a sci-fi movie. I was sure that after I left the next "customer" would be there to commune with the dead—or something equally as spooky.

Unprofessional was how it felt to me, but how could I imagine what professional should feel like? Even as a teenager, I remember thinking it was just weird. Little did I know the role this event would play later in my life.

"The first thing you have to do is relax. Free all of the tension from all of your muscles. Imagine that you are floating in a pool of saltwater. You are entirely weightless."

I did as I was told. I felt the stress and strain inside my body slip away. She continued giving me instructions, and slowly the thoughts that filled my waking mind started to evaporate into nothingness.

"What do you see, Glori?" she asked me.

"Nothing," I answered honestly.

"Good. Now I want you to think back to a day that happened several years ago."

"Okay."

"Now this was a horrible day, and you're going to see things that hurt and frighten you, but I want you to know that no matter what you see, you are safe. As long as you are here with me, you are completely safe, and nothing bad can happen to you. Do you understand that?"

"Yes."

My mom told me later that she asked me to recount the details of that fateful night when Wib first molested me. Under hypnosis, I recounted the details just as I did in my waking state. I told her everything that I remembered, and there were no new revelations. In other words, I told the same story, whether I was in or out of hypnosis.

At some point, while rehashing the abuse, I started to get upset and began to cry. True to the unprofessionalism of the process, the hypnotist didn't know how to handle my emotions. She seemed to realize then that this whole thing had gone too far, and that I wasn't prepared.

It was a bad, weird idea that turned out terribly, but in our minds, it had proven again that I was telling the truth. If hypnosis was an all-powerful way to get out the facts, then it was now clear. Right?

Wrong.

We were still under the mistaken belief that the truth mattered within the family. All that was left was for Wib to corroborate my story while under hypnosis. He must have believed in the mystical powers of hypnosis, too, because he never showed up. He agreed to at first, saying he had nothing to hide, but in the end, he didn't show.

We were hopelessly naïve to think Wib would keep his word about going to the hypnotist. Men who molest little girls aren't trustworthy people.

It didn't matter. Even if he had gone to the hypnotist and confessed everything, the family would not have changed their stance towards me.

CHAPTER 8

THE WARRIOR'S SOLITUDE

"Resilience depends on community and the stories we share."

— *Jean-Paul Bédard*

―――――

Bad Dreams

Most people hate their alarm clock.

For them, sleep is a respite or at least a safe and comfortable place. But an alarm clock ceases to be a petty nuisance when you relive your darkest fears each night.

The alarm clock was my saviour.

Dreams haunted me nearly every night—like the one where I'm sitting at the table in my grandmother's kitchen. I feel cold. A window is open. The frosty winter air is rushing in. I want to get up and close it, but I can't move. I look down, and I don't appear to be tied, but something keeps stopping me whenever I try to stand.

"Hello?" I cry out. "Is anyone here?"

All I hear is the hum of the refrigerator. The longer I sit, the colder the room gets. It doesn't take long for me to see my breath. I look down and see that my skin is starting to turn blue. I try to cry out again, but I'm now shivering so much I can't speak. Slowly, I feel the warmth that animates me fade entirely from my body. My heart stops beating. My lungs no longer take in any breath.

I'm dead, yet I see everything around me. I still feel the coldness. I hear the hum of the refrigerator. I watch as Wib walks into the kitchen, closes the window and reaches into a drawer. He pulls out a steak knife and studies it as if selecting the perfect tool.

Deciding it's precisely the needed weapon he walks back to the table, pulls up on the tablecloth and crouches down underneath.

Beep. Beep. Beep.

The alarm went off and saved me from finding out what he was going to do with that steak knife.

Or, there was a dream about the bridge. The setting was in Miramichi, where a wide river splits the town apart. Even in my waking hours, I didn't like that bridge. I had a fear that it was going to collapse every time I crossed it.

It didn't help that my dad was always distracted while driving across the river. He gawked and chattered away while I freaked out. I swear he shouldn't have had a licence.

In the dream, which recurred regularly, the bridge falls. My mom is on one side and my dad is on the other. It was entirely symbolic of my fears. I was put in the position of separation again. In my dream, I was asked to choose between my parents, something I never did in my real life. I always wanted both of them. Maybe I was the bridge in my dreams, and I was scared about myself falling apart.

What I do know is that sleep wasn't restful for me. Nightmares became a pattern of fear and anxiety that continued for years.

I had already pushed away Little Glori to become a warrior. It was a survival mechanism, but unsurprisingly, I was starting to experience the psychological consequences of this split. If I was scared in my sleep, I tried to be the opposite in my waking hours, and I started leaning heavily on my accomplishments as a source of strength.

Training Like a Warrior

Every survivor exhibits his or her symptoms. Some survivors fall apart while others appear to be the epitome of success. Once I became a warrior, I focused on my success to the point of obsession. I wanted to control everything that would happen to me for the rest of my life.

Step inside the mind of an obsessed 16-year-old survivor for a moment. It's early. The sun has yet to rise. No one else in the neighbourhood will be up for another two hours. They aren't in training, but I am. I wipe the sleep from my eyes and climb out of bed. Few things have changed since I sat crying on my dad's bathroom floor just a few years earlier, but now I have a goal.

When I was six, I learned the thrill that came from having a red ribbon pinned to my chest. That feeling compels me to set my clock early and grab a quick bowl of cereal while everyone else is asleep. The secret that early morning runners don't want you to know is how beautiful and peaceful the world is at that time of day. As the darkness fades to light, the only sounds come from your running shoes hitting the ground and your heart as it beats faster to keep up with exertion.

People confuse solitude with loneliness, but they are two entirely different feelings. Loneliness is a sensation that stays with you no matter where you are. A person can feel lonely sitting with 30,000 other people in a stadium. Solitude is a feeling of well-being and strength. Lonely always feels terrible; solitude is exhilarating. Lonely means feeling ignored and unwanted; solitude means feeling free of judgment and insecurity.

As important as they were for my training, those early morning runs allowed me to be at peace. That was the best. For part of my day I wasn't the angry girl who'd been abused by her step-grandfather. I was Glori, the runner who could beat anyone.

I'm a warrior, and running is my battlefield. Getting myself up early each morning to train is how I win the battle.

Vulnerability Comes Through

The rest of the day, I anticipated the other alarm I loved—the one that announced last class was over. It was time to hit the track to train again, this time under the tutelage of a great coach and one of my first positive role models other than my dad.

Fewer than five minutes after it rang, I would be in my green and white track uniform walking out of the girls' locker room and heading toward the field.

A year earlier, my dad had driven me to downtown Chatham where there was a little sporting goods store and bought me my first pair of cleats. Dad was a runner in his youth, just like me, so he knew the value of a good pair of cleats. I had been running competitively since grade six, but I felt like a real track athlete once I put on my cleats.

As time passed they got battered and scuffed, but they still fit. It was hard not to think of them as possessing a special kind of magic.

"You're late, Glori," joked my coach. His name was—and I swear I'm not making this up—John A. MacDonald, just like Canada's first prime minister.

I was always the first person on the field. Coach John A. worked with me beginning in grade nine. Aside from my dad, he was the most important man in my life. He made a living as a teacher but he made a life as a coach.

After Wib's abuse, I found it challenging to trust any man. Coach was the exception. With him, I felt safe. He had no ulterior motive beyond making me a better person. After having gone through so much, I'd mostly stopped believing there were good people in the world—Coach proved me wrong.

He was always honest with me—sometimes brutally—but I respected this because I understood that everything he did and said was for my benefit. He would never criticize to hurt me, only to make me stronger. I trusted him completely. If he told me to run off the end of a cliff, I'd do it. Fortunately, he never gave me anything but reliable guidance. I can't say enough good things. He had a massive impact on my life, and I'll be forever grateful for that.

In the life of an abused child, small things make a big difference. All it takes is one person, like Coach John A., to help a broken child see the beauty within them. One person can help a child dare to believe.

I maintained an unhealthy attachment to success and achievement, but Coach showed me that it was good to seek success. He showed me how to put my focus on the right things and that, with the proper support, I could do anything. Most afternoons were spent running the usual drills. I competed in the 100m hurdles, the 200m hurdles, the 400m hurdles, the 4x4 400m relay, and the long jump.

I was the shortest girl on the field in every one of those races. There were no exceptions to this rule. My competitors always looked me over and wondered how I managed to win on my little legs. They didn't know my secret—I ran every race as if it were my last.

I held nothing back. Going all out allowed me to win my races and set records, but it eventually proved to be my downfall. My zeal to win meant pushing myself past limits my small body could not handle. I suffered multiple physical injuries, many of which I kept to myself.

"What's on the schedule today, Coach?" I asked as I started stretching while we waited for the rest of the team to show up.

"Something a little different, Glori," he answered with a nod towards a group of younger kids who were walking across the field in the distance. I could tell they were from the nearby junior high school.

I knew enough not to say anything out loud, but inside, I let out a groan. Being at the track was my special time, and the last thing I wanted to do was waste it on a bunch of kids, even if some of them were only a year younger than I was.

Trying to find the bright side, I figured this would give me the chance to show off a little, which I was always happy to do. Five minutes later, everyone was there. To the casual observer, it would have been hard to tell the two groups apart, but when you're a teenager, one year might as well be 10.

Coach gave his usual speech about the importance of hard work and proper training, and how every race you finish is as important as every race you've won. I believed that first part, but always had my doubts about the second. Surely the races you won were more important, weren't they?

Soon I found myself explaining the proper hurdles technique to a group of six kids. In my case technique was vital, since I lacked long legs that could leap over hurdles effortlessly. It was about the right combination of timing and exertion. Most people don't realize that there's no penalty for knocking over a hurdle. As long as the hurdler doesn't do it deliberately, they could knock over every single one and still win. You just have to be the first person to cross the finish line.

Despite this fact, I always took it as a personal failure if I knocked over a hurdle—even if only at practice. I would feel shame every time it happened.

After explaining how to run hurdles, including an explanation of the mechanics of jumping each hurdle, I set up a couple of hurdles on the grassy infield. Then I prepared to demonstrate the process in front of my small audience. I would jump a set of three hurdles to give the kids an idea of how it worked. I'm not sure if it was the casual atmosphere that caused it, but the strangest thing happened.

I hit the second hurdle and fell face first.

You can imagine how mortified I was. Here I was, put in a position to teach for the first time—by the Coach I respected so much—and not only did I fail, I embarrassed myself in the process. It proved, and not for the last time, that I didn't necessarily have it all together. I was vulnerable, and even though I was a top hurdler at my school, things were going on below the surface that could make me crack.

Thankfully, Coach wasn't like so many of the critical and angry people I knew. He didn't hold it against me or make fun of me at all. Still, I could never let something like that happen to me again. As a teenager, my obsession with winning was growing. It would continue to get stronger.

CHAPTER 9

JEALOUSY AND ANGER

"I no longer had faith in myself or my own judgment. And when you come down to it, that's all a person has. Once it's gone, how do you get it back?"

— *Theo Fleury*

Looking for Acceptance

As much as I loved track, it wasn't my entire life. I spent the rest of my free time like any other teenager—with friends. I never liked being my actual age, so I always tried to compensate by acting older and by wearing my mom's clothes.

My circle of close friends included my stepfather Pete's two children, Tasha and Cassandra, as well as my schoolmates, Kerri-Lynn, Judy and Erin. As much as I enjoyed their company, I always felt a bit left out and lonely inside the group. I had told them about my abuse when I was younger—in about grade five or six—and their instinctual reaction was to ignore it, pretend like I never said anything and distance themselves. I can't blame them. They were kids, and no doubt didn't know what to think about it.

Because of the awkward silence, I always felt like somewhat of an outsider. I had shared my sincerest, darkest secret and, based on their reaction, it seemed like none of them cared. Looking back, I'm sure their response came out of discomfort, not a desire to hurt me. Still, it's hard to understand that as a teenager.

The exception was Judy. She and I talked about everything, and we have remained friends to this day. I'm grateful for our friendship. But every teenager knows the one-on-one dynamic is different than the group dynamic. It was in the group where I felt most uncomfortable.

I've since learned that you can't ask a survivor to be silent and then expect them to be comfortable. I was probably expecting too much from them.

Most adults aren't emotionally equipped to deal with these kinds of personal revelations, much less teenage kids.

Their apparent lack of concern served as another signal to me that the world did not want to understand my inner torment. People wanted me to remain silent – at least that's what I thought.

Boyfriends

My friends' apathy would have bothered me a lot more if I weren't frequently distracted by the adventure of my first romances.

Jeremiah came along in ninth grade. I liked him until I caught him cheating on me at the beach. He was the warm-up boyfriend before the big high school romance, but there was already a pattern forming with Jeremiah. I didn't see it at the time, but I was already choosing men in the same way my mom did.

In Grade 10, I fell for Rod, who was three years my senior. He was tall and slender, baby-faced and, most importantly, he made me laugh. I was in my car when I spotted him, and it was a classic case of love at first sight. He was already out of high school, getting ready to go to a trade school in Saint John.

As much as I loved him, I adored his family. Mine had always been so dysfunctional that I grew up not knowing sane and rational families existed. There never seemed to be any drama in Rod's house, which was why I spent as much time there as I could. Before long, I felt more like a part of their family than I did my own.

I especially loved going to his family's cottage, which was an hour away from Miramichi.

The relationship was a gift. I felt loved, and I had a lot of fun with Rod. Most importantly, I learned a lot about relationships. Rod knew about the abuse. He stayed with me and loved me anyway. I had a glimpse of what a great relationship could be. So, I had it. My perfect love life was now in order.

There was just one problem. As much as I knew he liked me, he couldn't be faithful. I never knew what he was up to, and this made me somewhat crazy. Everywhere I went with him I knew he'd slept with half of the town, and I was always wondering who in the room had also been with my boyfriend.

I couldn't control the past, but I resolved to make the future bend to my will. I became so fiercely protective of my relationship with Rod. I'd experienced much loss in my life, and with my commitment to controlling every aspect of my life, I didn't plan on experiencing loss in my love life, especially since I loved his family so much. I was fiercely protective of our relationship. Who am I kidding? I was jealous.

If I saw Rod talking to another girl—especially one I didn't trust or like—I felt extreme rage. I'm not someone that often resorted to violence, but when it came to Rod and the question of other girls, aggression was never far from my mind. In my head, losing Rod meant more than losing a boyfriend; it meant losing the only stable family life I had ever known.

Rod knew how upset his history made me and he did his best to keep it covered up, but whenever we went out in public, there was some joker who thought it would be hilarious to point out one of his old conquests and then watch the fireworks fly.

I wanted to believe that he'd get his life together and that we'd get married after high school, but I also couldn't get over his past. It caused me pain to know what a player he was. There were other things, too. I already knew at that age that I couldn't live in Miramichi. My plan was always to leave as soon as I could. I needed to get out of the shadow of my past to create the life I wanted. Rod was a local boy. He wasn't going anywhere.

I needed someone stable and grounded, not just a fun boy. I loved him, but he wasn't the one for me. The ultimate sign that he wasn't the guy for me was that my dad didn't like him. Dad held the vision for my life. He always told me I was going to do great things in the world, and he saw that my relationship with Rod was a potential roadblock on my path.

We ended it and went our separate ways. Maybe I wasn't going to follow the family pattern after all.

CHAPTER 10

TURNING THE CORNER

"We must accept finite disappointment,
but never lose infinite hope."

— Martin Luther King, Jr.

Recklessness Catches Up

The Monday of Victoria Day weekend had been circled on my calendar for a long time. Monday was the day of provincials, where the runners that would go on to nationals would be selected. It was the most important event of my life. Every Olympic dream I ever had would become reality. But, for the first time, an obstacle stood in my way.

I never learned her name, but I'll always remember her legs. They looked like they were carved out of marble, and they went up to her neck.

If this were a bad '80s sports movie, she'd inevitably be a Russian super-athlete who had been raised from birth to do nothing but win hurdles. Instead, this was real life, and she was just another competitive young girl who was driven to succeed as much as me. I recognized the look of obsession in her eyes.

"You nervous, Glori?" Coach asked me as we waited for my event to come up in the rotation.

"No," I lied.

"Really?"

"Uh-huh."

"Because it would be alright if you were. You've never lost, but you've also never faced this level of competition before."

"It's going to be fine. I'm not afraid of anyone here."

"Not even her?" he cocked his head toward the girl with the legs, who was stretching 50 feet away.

"She doesn't look that tough. I can beat her."

"Yes, you can. Remember that."

I looked around the crowd to see if I could catch any familiar faces. I knew everyone was out there, but I couldn't find them. I wasn't sure if knowing they were there made me more or less nervous. Then I saw my dad and flashed back to what he had said the last time he watched me race.

"Yes, you won, Glori," he said, stating a fact, not offering congratulations, "but you could have been faster. You could have won by more than what you did. You can never forget that. The day you do is the day you begin to lose."

I was mad at him for saying that to me. All I wanted to hear was what a good job I had done and how proud he was of me. But at that moment, a part of me felt like he was right. If I was going to win today, I had to be faster than ever before.

"Have a good race," I heard someone say. I turned and saw it was the girl with the legs. She spoke with a very thick francophone accent, which only managed to make her seem more ominous.

"You too," I said, offering up my hand, which she shook. Her grip was stronger than I expected. With that, she turned away. Looking back, I wish we had been able to have an actual conversation. I suspect we had a lot in common.

"Four hundred is up," said Coach. It was time for my event. I unzipped my track jacket and took off my pants. My blood was now pumping fast, and I was warm.

I took a deep breath and tried to calm my nerves. Remaining calm under pressure is an essential part of winning—something in which I excelled.

The five competitors walked over to the blocks. Fate placed the girl with the legs right beside me. I caught her glancing towards me, but I refused to grant her the same consideration.

"On your marks!"

We stepped into our blocks and crouched down.

"Get set!"

We rose up in the blocks and waited for that agonizing second to pass.

"Go!"

Both of us jumped out of the blocks with perfect starts and sailed in unison over the first hurdle. As much as I wanted to believe that all she had was muscle and height on her side, it was apparent that her technique was excellent. She was a true hurdler.

The other runners fell behind as the two of us leaped over the second hurdle. One of them would have to settle for third. As we jumped over the fifth hurdle, I thought I detected a tiny miscalculation on her part. No one else would have noticed it, but I took it as my opportunity to win this race.

As we made the turn towards the last half of the race, I looked up for less than a fraction of a second and felt my heart freeze in my chest. There was Wib, on the corner of one of the turns, staring at me. I thought I was hallucinating—given some of my bizarre dreams it wouldn't have been unlikely if I were. I looked up again to make sure, and there he was, cheering from the sidelines.

For an instant, I forgot about the race and the girl with the legs running beside me. Rage was on my mind. It consumed me. How dare he come here and ruin this for me? Today was my special day. He had no right to violate it with his presence. To this day, I don't understand the psychology of why he would show up there. Was it to deliberately mess with my mind? Or was it a calculation to make him look like he cared? Or, was it any number of other things?

I don't know for sure, but I do know that sexual abuse is about power. Showing up might have been another way to exercise his power over me. He said with his actions that he could commit crimes against me with impunity.

Seeing him served a critical purpose in my favour. I call it "rocket fuel." Starting from when I became a warrior, that night on my dad's bathroom floor, I could take negative situations and use them to fuel me to action. I couldn't give Wib the pleasure of seeing me crumble in front of him. I had to be stronger than I'd ever been before, so I used my rage to propel my feet forward.

I held nothing back. If this was the last race I ever ran, I was going to win it. By the ninth hurdle, I sensed I had a microscopic lead over my opponent, but even just one little mistake would mean the end of my lead. There was only one more hurdle to go, and then the finish line.

The hurdle came and went, and I was mere feet away from victory when I felt a searing pain erupt in my upper right leg. I ignored it and leaned forward as far as my body would allow. Upon crossing the finish line, I collapsed on the track in tears. I already knew I had torn a quadricep. The pain surged through my entire body. I couldn't hear the cheers of everyone around me or the congratulations of my fellow racers. I had won by inches.

Coach helped me up and took me to the sidelines where they threw an icepack on my leg and wrapped it with a tensor bandage. I kept waiting for him to say, "Good job, Glori," but he stayed silent.

The other events came and went. I picked up my medal and waited for the news that I was going to be joining the team representing

New Brunswick on the way to nationals. Instead, I found out why Coach hadn't been smiling.

"They've decided not to take you, Glori," he told me.

I knew that he would never, ever lie to me, but I couldn't help but assume this had to be a cruel joke. There was no other explanation for it.

"What?" I questioned.

"They were already worried you might be injury prone. Today's race convinced them. You're not going to nationals."

"But I won. I always win. I've never lost."

"They know that, but they're worried that you can only keep pushing yourself so much. At a certain point, you could permanently hurt yourself."

"So, who's going?"

"The girl who came in second."

"But I beat her."

"Yes, you did, but just barely and she's walking just fine. You may have won the race, but they feel she's the better athlete."

"But that's not fair!"

"It probably isn't, but they aren't going to change their minds."

He was right. They didn't. I spent that night sitting in the spectator stands on my school's sports field sobbing as hard as I ever had before. I had worked and trained so hard to go to nationals that I never once imagined it was even possible that it wouldn't happen—not even once.

I was too angry, and it was too soon for me to understand the irony of this moment. I had gotten as far as I had in track because I was willing to push my body past the breaking point to win. But just when it mattered the most, this recklessness caused me to lose out on the prize.

I won four gold medals that day and was named most outstanding athlete, but I was crushed.

I wish I could say I learned something from this, but it would take a few more decades before that would be true.

CHAPTER 11

THE PIZZA YEARS

"My attitude is that if you push me into something that you think is a weakness, then I will turn that perceived weakness into a strength."

— *Michael Jordan*

Going Through the Steps

The coaches' decision to leave me off the team for nationals changed my life.

I gave up running. It had been the most crucial part of my life for years. Once I realized it would never take me any further, I stopped and never went back. Even when I decided to focus on my health in my 30s, I turned to yoga.

To this day, it's hard for me to think about track and field. I loved running, and to have my greatest potential taken away was painful. Running was my sport because it was all about my effort. I didn't have to rely on anyone else. My hard work tipped the odds in my favour. Hard work fit my warrior persona.

I played field hockey, but I didn't like it much because of having to rely on others. From junior high on I had dreamed of going to York University, where Ben Johnson had trained before earning a 1984 Olympic bronze medal in the men's 100m sprint. When he lost his 1988 gold medal to a steroid scandal, I remained convinced it was the right place for me to go.

I changed my mind after the track meet. It no longer mattered where I went to school, as long as it got me away from Miramichi. After considering my options, I decided to study business at Dalhousie University in Halifax, Nova Scotia. It was in the Maritimes, which made it feel like a safe choice while still being in another city and province, which made it feel like I was finally away from my family.

By this time, my father had become independently wealthy through his real estate investments. I decided my independence meant too much to me to ask anyone—even my dad—to pay my tuition. I applied for student loans, assuming I would have to take on part-time jobs along the way to support myself.

I found myself assigned to Eliza Ritchie Hall; a big blue co-ed dorm built just a few years earlier. As soon as I walked into my dorm room, I felt like a new person. No one here knew me. I was free to re-create myself, as I wanted to be.

I was free for the first time in my life.

Freedom was the essence of my university experience. It was more than the studies, more than the opportunity. It was the sense that I could now do what I wanted in my life—even small things like being able to decorate my room or having a movie night with friends were big things to me. I was out of the shadow of my past. The toxic environment of my family and my several years of forced silence were behind me. I loved the freedom and was on my way to creating the life of which I had long dreamed.

Most importantly I was able to be a kid again. I still had my warrior persona, but in the freedom of not being attached to stigma and smothered by a dysfunctional family environment, I was able to let loose in a way I never knew before.

I was having fun, but as I was to find out eventually, fun isn't a magical cure for trauma.

Everything wasn't perfect in my new world. I made an enemy that first day—residence food. If you have ever lived on a university campus, you know what I mean. Never a big fan of high school cafeteria food, I used my training as an excuse to bring lunch from home instead. Unfortunately, I didn't train anymore, and I had to face this horrible food for breakfast, lunch and dinner—every day of the week.

Something had to change immediately.

My first solution was finding creative new ways to make Kraft Dinner. Only one communal microwave for the 92 residents meant some imagination was required. On the nights when we had spending money, we would make our way to the Dairy Deli, where pizza was available by the slice or by the box. They also had delectable donairs, and I ate them by the truckload.

Every student in Halifax was familiar with "Pizza Corner," a stretch of restaurants that stayed open late at night to capitalize on the hordes of hungry, drunken students stumbling home from the clubs. In every bar, you could buy a shot for $0.75 and a double for $1.25. The problem was the bars were all located down-hill from the four schools. Patrons faced a serious hassle when it was time to leave. The pizza we devoured wasn't just a late-night snack; it was a necessary carb-load for the uphill climb back to our dorms.

You can guess what this new diet did to me as the months progressed. When a first-year university student puts on weight, people call it the "Freshman 15," but in my case, it was the "Freshman 30."

Having gone from a whippet-thin athlete who spent every spare hour in training to a sedentary student devoted to the consumption of junk food, it's incredible I only gained 30 pounds rather than 100. I wish I could say that this sudden weight gain was my trade-off for excellent grades, but I was devastated to discover that university was much more rigorous than I had expected.

In high school, I had decent to very good grades because I was a reward-driven hard worker, but something happened when I got to Dalhousie. Like many freshmen, the study methods I had relied on no longer seemed to work. Content was coming so fast and furious that I didn't feel like I could keep up. Just taking excellent notes didn't guarantee I'd understand what I recorded when it came time to study.

I failed the first test of my life in Economics 101. I was devastated. For someone who hated to lose, a bad grade wasn't close to the feeling of coming in second. It was more like tripping in the blocks. The devastation was aggravated by my move to Halifax. Independence was less transformational than I had hoped. Yes, I loved the fresh start, and I was having more fun than ever, but the old trauma stayed with me. I escaped Wib's abuse but not the effects.

I didn't realize that I would never be able to shake the anxiety brought on by the abuse until I started genuinely healing. I used the fun of university to block the pain rather than deal with it. Rather than going away, the pressures of school and my "adult" lifestyle exacerbated the anxiety. The combination of my first real failure, feelings of isolation and easy access to cheap booze were leading to an emotional breakdown—it was only a matter of time until it happened.

The perfect storm blew in one night at a party in another Dalhousie residence. A bunch of us had already hit the bars to take advantage of ridiculously cheap shots and bought some more on the way. That night, I was wasted before we even arrived at the party. A few hours later, I was as drunk as I'd ever been.

Not good.

Like some abuse survivors, I'm not a happy drunk.

Some people say we become our true selves when intoxicated. Many survivors drink to numb the pain, but in my case, alcohol magnifies the pain. Dark memories I keep stowed away in the back of my mind leap to the forefront, and I find it impossible to concentrate on anything else.

That night I felt terrified and alone as I staggered around the strange building. It was filled almost entirely with people I didn't know. Stumbling along a hallway, I noticed a large man walk past me. On reflection, he couldn't have been older than 21, but in my drunk, anxious and traumatized state he was a dead ringer for Wib. The sight of him caused me to lose all control.

I became hysterical, screaming and crying. Within seconds I was surrounded by a group of concerned people.

"It's okay. It's okay. Calm down. Calm down," one young man spoke to me as if he was addressing a sobbing child who had just cut her knee playing.

"What's wrong? What's wrong?" he continued.

Mascara smudged across my face. I looked like a monster. Several minutes passed until my screams simmered down to quiet sobs and he was finally able to get through to me.

"What's your name?" he asked. Somehow, I managed to tell him.

"Okay, Glori. Whatever happened, you're safe now. I need you to tell me what's wrong."

"He won't leave me alone," I told him. "He keeps touching me. He told me he was going to kill my mom and sister if I told on him."

I heard someone say, "I think she was raped."

"Did someone hurt you, Glori?" asked the young man.

"Uh-huh," I nodded.

"Who was it? Who hurt you?"

"Wib!"

"Does anyone here know a Wib?" he turned and asked everyone close to me.

"I know an Albert," answered a guy close to him.

"Was the person who hurt you named Albert or Wib?" the man turned back and asked me.

"Wib!" I answered angrily.

"Maybe it's some guy who doesn't go to school here," suggested a voice.

"Glori, how do you know Wib?" asked the man.

"He's my... my... my... grandfather," I answered him between sobs.

"Your grandfather?"

"He won't leave me alone! He comes into the bathroom whenever I take a bath. He touches me! He tells me we're going to play a game, but I don't like it!"

"Is Wib here now?"

"He's right there!" I screamed, pointing to the poor kid whose remote resemblance set me off.

"That's your grandfather?"

"Yes!"

I saw him whisper something to someone close. That person then walked away and whispered something to my "grandfather." The two of them then walked away.

"Your grandfather's gone now, Glori," the man told me. "He's not going to hurt you. None of us are going to let him. Now I need you to help us find someone you know so they can take you home. Can you do that? We'll help you walk. Is that going to be okay?"

I nodded tearfully as he and someone else grabbed my sides and helped me stumble down the hallway. It only took a few minutes to find someone I recognized. Though she barely knew me, she was kind enough to take me back to our dorm and watch over me as I spent hours vomiting, before placing me in my bed.

You can guess how much fun it was to wake up the next morning. To this day, I wonder if someone slipped something into my drink.

Following in Mom's Footsteps

Luckily, word of my residence party freak-out didn't spread. As time passed, the distance between Rod and me grew, and I started having more serious relationships.

When it came to picking boyfriends, I followed my mom's example and went after big, handsome and muscular types who looked good from a distance but proved to be much less desirable the longer I knew them. You'd think my experiences as a kid would keep me far, far away from these kinds of guys, but I couldn't resist men who I thought could protect me.

Mel was the best example. I met him at JJ's, a local Halifax bar. We were both drunk, and I probably had a slight edge in that department. I was out with a bunch of girlfriends. We made a game of judging the "talent," trying to determine who was the hottest.

As I scanned the bar in my drunken haze, my eyes fell on a slab of muscle that was standing about 20 feet away. He was the most handsome man I'd ever seen—like something from a cheesy romance novel. After so many shots, it wouldn't have mattered if he'd been a young Brad Pitt or George Clooney, I was going to make my move.

Whatever I said to him must have clicked, because we exchanged phone numbers and he called me a few days later. We arranged a date. It was clear that with our beer-goggles lifted, he was slightly less impressed with me. I was still carrying my freshman weight gain, and he noticed. He was even more gorgeous than I remembered. This first date was also going to be our last.

But then he called me again and asked me to go out a second time. In retrospect, it's pretty clear why he chose to go out with an insecure girl like me. In the beginning, we had great chemistry. I liked the fact that he bought me presents every month. As time went on, I began to see that he wasn't as perfect as he appeared. The reason he looked so good was that he practically lived in the gym. He worked out every day and knew the name of every muscle in his body and how much time and effort he had put into developing them. The self-absorption should have been a red flag, but I was in no place to trust my instincts or read the signs.

I felt insecure and slightly inferior, so I let him push me around and accepted his routinely selfish behaviour. Another reason I stuck around far longer than I should have was because his family lived in Halifax. I was eager to adopt them as my own. But his family wasn't any better than he was.

His dad was a cab driver and his mom stayed home. Every Friday, we went to Mel's apartment, and the family would order one medium donair pizza. Between myself, Mel, his siblings and his parents, there was just enough for everyone to have a single piece.

I was working three different jobs at the time—waitressing at the University Club, clerking at Royal Bank, and selling shoes at Lady Foot Locker—all while going to school. His parents believed I had a lot of trauma coming from a broken home and would never be good enough for their son. In their eyes, he was a perfect angel who could do no wrong, while I was the one responsible for everything bad that happened in the world.

Eventually, it got so out of hand that I couldn't sweep it under the rug as "just one of those things." As handsome as Mel was, I had to admit that staying with him was toxic to my well-being. I wanted to date someone who let me have my own opinions, who didn't lecture me about every bite of food I put into my mouth and whose family wasn't more messed up and insane than my own. I didn't want an overbearing, over-dominant type of man.

But because of his temper, I kept my plans to myself until the school year ended, and I went back home for the summer. With a safe distance between us, I broke up with him over the phone. I never called him again.

I'm sure Mel's parents were relieved.

A Wolf in Sheep's Clothing

That summer, I decided it was time to make a change. I'd been self-conscious about the extra pounds I'd put on during my first year of university. Breaking up with Mel was the motivation I needed to get back into fighting shape. Mel always criticized my looks, believing my weight reflected poorly on him. I couldn't think of any better revenge than returning to Halifax with the kind of body that would drive him insane. Probably not the best reason to lose weight, but it was all the motivation I needed at the time.

Through diet and exercise, I got back to my high school weight and returned to Dalhousie feeling like I owned the universe. All I had to do was find a deserving guy to go out with this new, amazing version of me. Along came Kevin, the textbook example of the cliché that some things are too good to be true.

I met Kevin the same way I met Mel—in a noisy bar.

By the end of the week, we went on our first official date—dinner—where I learned all about him. He told me that he went to St. Mary's on a volleyball scholarship.

Of all my boyfriends, Kevin was the most traditionally romantic. He would buy me flowers and lay rose petals on the floors at my place. It didn't take long for me to start planning a future with him. I even got to know his parents and liked them. And I love his mom now, remembering that it was her who inadvertently tipped me off to the kind of guy Kevin was.

We were having dinner with his parents one night when his mom mentioned something about his high school transcripts arriving. I thought it was weird that a guy already in university, and playing for the volleyball team, would need his high school transcripts. With some intelligent questioning, I gathered that he hadn't graduated from high school yet! It slowly dawned on me that he fabricated the entire story about going to St. Mary's and having a volleyball scholarship.

Kevin seemed sweet and romantic, but even insecure me knew that blatant fabrication of an entire life story is a dangerous sign. He looked like a big step up from Mel, but he turned out to be the same type in a different costume. Our break-up left me wondering if I would ever be able to trust another man again.

I rode the merry-go-round for a while, shuffling through boyfriends like a deck of cards until I woke up to the gift of an extraordinary man that would eventually become my husband.

CHAPTER 12

PRAYERS ANSWERED

"Prayer is not asking. Prayer is putting oneself in the hands of God—at His disposition—and listening to His voice in the depth of our hearts."

— *Mother Teresa*

Keeping my Faith

In spite of their actions, my family thought of themselves as religious. Whether they were or not depends on your definition of religion. If going through the motions of a set of rituals is religious, then yes, we were a religious family. My mom was Anglican and regularly attended church on Sundays, while my dad was Catholic and rarely went to church.

I think being religious means acting out of love for your fellow man, woman and child. My family often failed on that front. Religion was an image to them. They had no interest in reality, truth or love. Years later, when my abuser died, I discovered just how vital this image was to them. All of the abuse was glossed over, and Wib's obituary only contained mention of what a great and "God-loving" man he had been.

There were aspects of religion that never resonated with me. The dogmatic crowd seems to think God is some picky old man, dictating what foods we should eat and getting pissed off when we break a random set of rules. I never liked being told what to believe. Since my parents went to different churches, believing in one particular version of religion didn't make much sense to me. I always seemed to be in limbo between Mom and Dad.

I don't claim to be religious, but I've always maintained faith in my life, even when I had no good reason. But what is faith, if not the belief that things are happening for a reason, and trusting in God that things will turn out as they should?

I had many good reasons to abandon God and my faith, but I remained a believer. Religion and church ritual always seemed like a sham, as I was made to sit beside Wib. This was horrifying, especially since I had to sit beside him after the abuse had ended and everyone knew. It was part of a game my family played called, "Let's Pretend This Never Happened." The pretending might have done as much damage to my soul as the actual abuse. Silencing my voice made things worse—much worse.

Being exposed to religion while sitting in church beside my abuser every Sunday might have been enough to make me give up on God and move on. However, I always kept faith as a part of my life. I prayed to God and believed in Him in spite of the horrors and trauma.

Our church had a weekly ritual that I perceived as being more spiritual than religious, and I always participated. At the end of the service, the pastor would ask, "Who wants to be saved today?" Tiny me would go to the front. I was the only kid, further cementing my reputation as a weirdo.

"Put your arms up and let in the light of Jesus Christ," the pastor would say. I prayed for the abuse to stop during the ritual. Each week I went back home to continued sexual abuse at the hands of my step-grandfather, and I'd tell myself a little story about how I must not have been good enough to deserve God's salvation.

During the cover-up years, I used the weekly ritual to pray for someone to believe me. My aunts and uncles worked together to keep my abuse quiet. With me being called a slut, a bitch and a liar, I felt unloved in my own family. All I wanted was to be believed.

It seems crazy that I cared so much about them in hindsight, but at that age, and for several years after, I just wanted a family. I just wanted to be loved. I didn't know any different.

My mom believed me and told me she loved me. She's had a big heart and always wanted the best for me. Still, she was unable to help me much, and her efforts at playing the middle often caused more damage than they resolved. After all, siding with us meant cutting herself, Bobbie and me off from the rest of the family. She needed approval from her family as desperately as I did, so she couldn't cut herself off from them. My need for family approval eventually changed into resentment for them.

As my need for approval diminished, my expectations shifted. My prayers changed, too. I started praying just to be loved unconditionally by one person. As simple as that prayer sounds, I'd never really experienced it.

On God's Time

God doesn't always answer prayers instantly. He certainly didn't answer my prayers the moment I made them. In reflection, I believe God helped me become an advocate. He wanted me to make significant changes, so God took the horrors of my sexual abuse, including the painful cover-up, and gave me a voice. Due to my tribulations, I know the survivors' pain. Healing the broken-hearted is a part of God's plan for me.

I would later start Little Warriors as a place where sexually abused boys and girls could be made whole. Would Little Warriors exist if I hadn't experienced the pain? I can never know for sure, but I don't believe so. The pain was intense enough that I couldn't sit back and do nothing. I had to do something. My pain became the burning desire behind Little Warriors. I was going to become an agent of change.

I didn't suffer abuse, the cover-up and the years of severe anxiety, PTSD and emotional pain to sit idly by. I experienced a taste of what so many survivors suffer through with some of my lousy university relationships.

I already had a glimpse of an abusive marriage when I dated Mel. He was controlling in everything he did, and his family treated me like a second-class citizen from the moment they met me. With Kevin, I was lied to and deceived. Sadly, many young women take this to be the norm and continue in relationships predicated on lies. Mel and Kevin weren't the answer to my prayers of being loved unconditionally. However, I managed to get through the relationships with the wrong men and eventually met a man who did love me unconditionally.

My prayers were answered, and not a moment too soon. I give God credit for that, but I also take my share of the credit. I wanted true love and respect in my life. I drew a line in the sand and set out to discover a great one.

Introducing Gary

Gary was unlike the other men whom I dated. The others were controlling and manipulative; Gary was loving and respectful. The others were in a rush to get me in bed, but Gary focused on the relationship. The story of our attraction, dating and marriage was unlike any other relationship. Heck, Gary was drastically different from anything I'd ever experienced. If you saw my life as a black-and-white movie, he would be the one character in full colour.

Gary wasn't just different than my other boyfriends. His family was different from any of the other people in my life. Unlike my driven and inattentive father, Gary exuded a quiet, balanced focus. Unlike my fearful and distracted mother, Gary and his family loved me unconditionally and treated me like a daughter. Unlike the angry, controlling and violent adult men I grew up around,

Gary and his dad were both strong without being macho. He was so different that I didn't know how to take him at first. Thank God I chose to invest in our relationship rather than run.

Gary and I were both students in the Faculty of Commerce at Dalhousie University. Through the admiration of mutual friends and by seeing how he carried himself, I developed a respect for Gary. He had a nice body (he always took care of himself), but even so, I didn't feel an immediate spark with him.

Perhaps it was because my dating radar was fixed on domineering and rude men, but I didn't see him for what he would eventually become. In spite of my lack of understanding he and I developed a friendship. Slowly, answers came to my prayers. Our first real connection took place when there was a group work project in one of our classes. I saw my opportunity to get to know Gary better—you know, as a friend.

"Hey Gary, come join our group," I shouted across the room to him.

He happily joined us.

Over the next couple of years, our friendship developed. We hung out occasionally and had several mutual friends in common. We got along fabulously and supported each other whenever needed. It wasn't until a couple of years after our meeting and a couple of events that I began to see him in a different light. Perhaps the better way to say it is that I began to understand my true feelings.

Looking back, I see that, while I might not have consciously known I had feelings for Gary, subconsciously, I was deeply in love with him. I didn't understand a relationship based on love and mutual respect. Just as it's hard to understand a foreign language the first time you hear it, it's hard to see love the first time you experience it.

At the time of my breakup with Kevin, I was working in accounts payable at Dalhousie. I'll never forget the moment that Gary came in to see me after the breakup. He'd brought a little Aladdin

Genie figurine and a letter for me as a gift. The letter said, "You're a great girl. You'll get over this, so get on with your life and follow your dreams."

I often joke that I'm in the remedial program when it comes to learning lessons and advancing myself spiritually and emotionally. My remedial progress was on full display that day when I was stunned and touched by Gary's beautiful gift, as I didn't see the love we had for each other. I remember thinking, "Wow, what a great guy." My conscious mind still didn't believe it could work. Something was starting to shift in me, though, and it was now inevitable that we'd get together, even if I didn't yet know it.

The second event that shifted me was when Gary broke up with his girlfriend. I'd been on some dates with random guys after my breakup with Kevin, but I hadn't gotten a new boyfriend in the meantime. I was at my place one evening getting ready for one of those blind dates when Gary called.

"It's over," he said.

"What's over?" I asked.

"We broke up," he replied.

I'll never forget my reaction to the news. It was the first time my conscious mind connected with my subconscious. As Gary told me he'd broken up with his girlfriend, I tilted the phone away from my mouth and whispered, "YES!" as I furiously fist pumped. It shocked me because as a good friend, I wanted to be supportive of him.

In a flash, I realized that I wanted him for myself. I've learned through my journey that the mind can lie, but the heart and soul tell the truth. The fist pump was the body speaking. To this day, if I start losing my connectedness, or if I start slipping back into old patterns of self-abuse or ego-driven behaviour, it's my body that reacts first—before my mind.

Trusting the Process

It wasn't long until we made it official and started dating exclusively. The groundwork of friendship was laid over the previous two years; now, our most significant task was intimacy. With my self-destructive tendencies influencing me, I still had a few lingering doubts about Gary.

I expected a rough and tumble "manhandling" both emotionally and physically from men. I was too inexperienced to understand that strength didn't look like that. Gary was not the manhandling type. He was loving and gentle, and he was always in the relationship for the long haul, even though I didn't understand it for a while. I finally had the one person who loved me—an answered prayer. Still, I couldn't see the gift in its entirety. Thank God I chose to stay and see if the proverbial sparks would fly once a strong relationship was in place.

Fly they did, eventually.

I expected Gary would become aggressive the moment he had me alone, but the reality was much different. We developed intimacy, without sex. Gary was so romantic and caring. He'd run me a bath, fill it with bubbles and then let me enjoy my bath, alone. He was great, but I wanted some action! I practically had to throw myself at him, but eventually, the physical attraction was in place.

Looking back, I know that Gary was more aware of my fragility around love and intimacy than I was. His tender, caring approach was what I needed. I chose intimacy over forced acts at the hands of Wib or the belittling treatment from domineering men in my past.

The love of my life was in place, and it wasn't long before we were deepening our relationship.

CHAPTER 13

WESTWARD WE GO

"You'll learn, as you get older, that rules are made to be broken. Be bold enough to live life on your terms, and never, ever apologize for it."

— *Mandy Hale*

Getting Serious

Gary and I became a full-time couple by October 1994, which was our final year of university. Things happened quickly from there. Within a month, he invited me to meet his parents in Yarmouth, Nova Scotia, an eight-hour drive from Chatham, N.B.

I must have been madly in love, because I made the drive to Yarmouth by myself in a horrific East Coast snowstorm, at night, in my tiny Mazda RX-7. It wasn't the safest of journeys, but I was dangerously in love, and any risk seemed reasonable.

Upon arriving in Yarmouth, it didn't take me long to be shocked by Gary and his family. As I neared the end of my drive I saw Gary. He was awaiting my arrival, standing by his car at a T-turn intersection. My heart melted at that moment. After leading me home, we parked in the driveway of their gorgeous and quaint little home.

How can I explain Gary and his family? They were normal. Normal doesn't begin to describe them. They were functional and loving, but that's not necessarily normal. Gary's family was the epitome of caring. I've never met kinder, more compassionate, more caring people. They lived in a quaint old home, with the smell of baked bread never too far away. They sat together in the morning drinking coffee while speaking to each other in calm and loving voices. They cared for each other, and it showed in their actions. There was only one thing out of place.

Me.

I didn't fully believe them. With my background, I naturally assumed the closets would be overflowing with skeletons and that demons resided in the cracks in the floor. For a brief time, I believed it was all a clever cover-up, put on for my benefit.

I'll never forget the incredulous look on Gary's face when I asked him, "Ok, where are the child molesters, where are the alcoholics, where is the physical and emotional abuse? Who is doing it, and what's going on? Level with me."

"What are you talking about?" was his classic, understated response. By the look on his face, I thought maybe I sprouted a second head. By his response, I knew there was no cover-up. He was genuinely shocked by the question.

What I saw in Gary's family was genuine. Once I got over my disbelief, I saw the beauty. I fell in love with Gary's parents. In many ways, they became my parents from that day on. As much as I loved them, they loved me back in equal amounts. There was no way that Gary could have gotten rid of me after that moment. I even told Gary's mom that weekend that I was going to marry him.

The love I received from the Meldrum family shocked me because I still saw myself as damaged goods. It would be several years until I learned to love myself, yet they loved me from day one. I credit their love with guiding me slowly and caringly down that path of personal discovery and self-compassion. It speaks volumes about Gary's family's loving nature when a damaged young woman can show up at their home with strong intentions for their son, yet they only saw the good in me. If they saw the dysfunction, they hid it well and knew I could overcome it.

They knew me better than I knew myself. Once I'd fallen in love with Gary's parents, our relationship went to another level, very quickly. There was an unspoken certainty to our future from that point on.

Having 'The Talk'

About a month after the trip to Yarmouth to meet Gary's parents, I took him back to Miramichi to meet my mom. It was Christmas break, and we stayed in the spare bedroom of my mom's tiny apartment. Gary and I were lying there together one night, and it must have been the influence of my mom's apartment living conditions that drove me to speak so frankly about the future with Gary.

"I'm heading out west the moment I'm finished my last class. I'm not even waiting for convocation," I said.

"Okaaaayyyy," replied Gary.

"I want you to come with me," I said.

"Okay," replied Gary again.

"I want to be with you, but there's no way I'm staying here, so if you want to be with me, you have to come with me," I said.

Naturally, he had mixed emotions. He wanted to be with me as much as I wanted to be with him, but this was all very sudden, and he loved his family. Gary picked up the phone immediately and called his dad to ask what he thought about his son moving west.

"I've always wanted the best for you, and I've always wanted you to move when you were old enough," said Gary's dad.

As beautiful as the Maritime provinces are, and as important as family ties were to Gary's dad, he knew that for Gary to make a better life, he had to go where the opportunity was. The beautiful and quaint East Coast lacked real possibilities. Western Canada was the place to find ample opportunity. The chance to be far away from the dysfunction of my extended family and my abuser drove me to leave at the first moment possible.

I had to get out of there so I could be free from them. I had to get out of there so I could be a big success and show everyone that I was okay. Gary knew the opportunity was in the west, too. We decided that moment in my mom's apartment.

We were moving west.

Wrapping Things Up, Starting New

The next few months passed in a blur. We finished our degree requirements, got our resumes together and organized the logistics of the trip. I sold my Mazda RX-7 for $3,000. Gary and I got credit cards with $500 limits, and we sent out eight boxes of clothes ahead of us. Our destination was Vancouver where we'd make all of our dreams come true.

We wrote our last exams near the end of April 1995. A few days later, we flew over the vast forests and prairies of Canada. We had grand expectations for our lives, expecting to make outstanding money and live like the rock stars we thought we were. We had one little stopover to make in Alberta before we could get down to the serious business of success and happiness in Vancouver. My Aunt Fern lived in the town of Drayton Valley with her husband, Dan. She heard of our big plans to move west, so she urged us to stop by and stay with her and her family for a couple of weeks before starting our life in Vancouver.

Since she offered to pay for us to change our tickets, we couldn't say no. In spite of the family difficulties, I retained a relationship with Aunt Fern. She was there the day the rest of the family called me a slut, a whore and a liar. She and Dan didn't partake in the name-calling, and Fern even took me out of the room when things got too crazy. There was an uneasy understanding between us. More accurately, she participated in pretending the abuse never happened, and as long as I kept my mouth shut, she was okay with it.

I was happy to stay with Fern, Dan and their kids in Drayton Valley before heading to Vancouver. We didn't expect to fall in love with her kids and fall in love with Alberta. Fern and Dan told us about Alberta's opportunities, and although it was landlocked, the rural lifestyle reminded us of a little bit of back east.

Dan took us to see Calgary and Edmonton, and we were impressed by everything. Still, we planned to live in Vancouver. Old Canada in the East had been sending people to New Canada in the West for a century, but no other place had the romantic appeal of Vancouver. So, we stuck to our plan.

After our fun stint in Drayton Valley with Fern and Dan, the reality of the Vancouver lifestyle collided directly with the fantasy. For us, small-town East Coasters, the vast, busy, multicultural and expensive Vancouver lifestyle was a little too much. We were overwhelmed from the moment we arrived, but in the "can do" spirit of our youth, we gave it a try for three weeks.

Not Fitting In

My first interview was at a major pizza corporation, where I was seeking a career in the marketing department.

"Nobody hires juniors. You'll never get a job in Vancouver with that resume," said my interviewer. It made me wonder why they'd called me in the first place. Gary faced the same problems, as our resumes were similar.

Our prospects dimmed.

Another crack appeared in our master plan when we realized Aunty Elsie and her husband didn't have the perfect West Coast life we'd imagined. We planned to live with them until we got on our feet. The Vancouver lifestyle is obscenely expensive, while at the same time provides less in the way of income. It became apparent to Gary and me that Elsie and her husband didn't get along so well, and it didn't take us too long to figure out why.

They were under enormous financial pressure. They were living in a modest home, which costs a lot of money in Vancouver, and the financial stress affected their relationship. Housing and a million other expenses meant, even though they had good jobs, they were struggling to keep financially healthy. Another thing we didn't love about the city was the rain. It started the moment we arrived and never stopped. It wasn't long before Gary and I were having another late-night conversation in bed.

I started talking about the city, but Gary quickly interjected, "I hate it here."

"I hate it here, too," I replied.

Just as quickly as we decided to move to Vancouver five months earlier, we immediately resolved to leave. We were only there for two hard weeks. We hustled, it rained, we saw the reality for what it was, and we knew it wasn't what we wanted.

Where was the opportunity we expected? Vancouver wasn't full of it, and the drizzle was killing us.

Dealing With Reality

Luckily for us, we had seen Alberta only a couple of weeks earlier. There we saw a glimpse of the life we wanted. Alberta was quieter, simpler, and slower than Vancouver, yet the opportunity was higher there. We fixed our sights on Alberta and said sayonara to Vancouver.

The only choice left was between Calgary and Edmonton. We decided on Edmonton, as we fell in love with the river valley and the smaller feel of the city. We could never have imagined the life we would build there.

Vancouver didn't work out, but we still had dreams of grandeur. We thought Edmonton was just the place for us to set up shop. Edmonton looked like a promised land of untold riches for us. However, there was still a little thing called "reality" to face.

First, we were both juniors—extreme juniors—and it's always been hard to get a high-income job as a junior, even in a strong economy.

Second, we didn't have much money. It was a countdown until we would be flat broke. Oh, and we had substantial student loan debt that we needed to start repaying. My first job interview with West Edmonton Mall looked promising. The position came down to one other candidate and me. The other guy won. I'd have to remain on the shelf for a little bit longer.

We got a small apartment in the meantime and purchased all of the furniture for $100 at a garage sale. For this price tag, we even got a hide-a-bed. I'll never forget the hide-a-bed because it had springs sticking out of it. I probably still have scars on my back from that thing.

Life wasn't glamorous, but we were thrilled to have a place to call home. It was a little love nest, and with $60,000 in student loan debt, no jobs and no money, it's a miracle we could even get an apartment. It was called Fairmont Village and we signed a lease at an affordable price. Along with our gross little hide-a-bed, we also had a $10 TV on its last legs, and several other "vintage" appliances and furniture.

My job search floundered for some time, although Gary secured a job—as a repo man. One could say that the role was a bad fit for Gary. Gary is not a small man, but he's no Hells Angels biker either. He looks nothing like the repo men you see on TV. Repossessing cars was not his calling, and he regularly had angry people, often in trouble with the law, threaten him.

In addition to the dangerous work conditions, Gary was forced to take two buses and a taxi to get to work. Edmonton is a driver's city, and this combination of public transportation took an hour and a half each way. It was an awful job, but it was all we had at the time.

I'll never forget the time I was sitting at home in the middle of the day watching depressing soap operas. I couldn't find a job to save my life, which was beyond rare for me. I'm a hustler and have never struggled with pounding the pavement to make things happen. Still, there I sat.

Frustrated, I began to question our decision to move to Edmonton. Wallowing in self-pity, I heard a loud "POP!" as our television stopped working. My eyes filled with tears as smoke filled the living room. The poor little $10 TV gave up the ghost. Even a lifeless electronic box couldn't stand to live like this.

In my exaggerated state, it was just too much. It symbolized all of our more significant problems. I called Gary in despair. He must've thought I was close to the edge as I sobbed into the phone about the poor broken TV. Gary never gave any indication that he thought I was nuts. Instead, he reassured me that everything would be okay. Then he did the sweetest thing in the world.

Coming home from work, he went out of the way from his already arduous journey and purchased a TV from Sears. He paid for it on credit. Gary is financially responsible and always has been, but my phone call was enough to make him pull out his credit card. I think we both understood what the TV represented. It was a very Gary-like act of love, and it worked. He made me feel safe and hopeful all at the same time. I resolved to get myself out of the house and keep pounding the pavement.

If Gary could push through this struggle, so could I.

On the Warpath

Thanks to Gary's loving nudge, it wasn't long before I was back on the warpath. This little warrior hadn't been defeated, and she wasn't about to be now. I decided that I needed to get my foot in the door somewhere. I knew I would have to lower my expectations (temporarily) about the type of work I would do, so I ended up at a recruitment agency. I just needed a start.

I still dreamed of a job in marketing, but I knew it was time to try something else to get rolling. At the agency, I met a great guy named Greg, who I still keep in touch with today. He believed in my potential.

"Listen, nobody takes on juniors, but why don't you come work here for me?" he said.

It wasn't the dream job I coveted, but it was a job. Gary carried us long enough with his terrible job repossessing vehicles. It was time I got to work, so I took the job. I had a sinking feeling when he told me the beginning salary was $22,000 per year. It crushed my dreams.

I had such grandiose visions about the kind of money I'd make when I left university. This reality was drastically different. Not only was I not in my field, I was earning a pittance. Still, it was a start. The fighter in me was alive and well, and I knew I could build upon it. I went to work on the industrial desk, also known as the worst desk of all (especially in the industrial city of Edmonton).

Now and then, an exciting position would come up, and some of the candidates were good. More often, though, I was putting drunks to work for a day, a week, or however long they could work before sabotaging themselves. Every day I took calls from rough men saying things like, "I spent the night in jail for beating up my wife. I need to go to work."

To this day, I'm grateful to Greg for giving me the opportunity, but for my sanity, I couldn't stay long. I spent eight months there, hating every minute of it before moving on. I told them I was going to do my MBA, and politely made my exit.

I never did my MBA, but I had to get out of there. I don't advocate lying, so I'm not exactly proud of the story I made up. At the time, I was still surviving. Making up that little story was part of my survival.

I quickly found another job with a radio station based in St. Albert. We lived on the south side of Edmonton at the time. If you don't know the city, this meant I traveled the entire length from south to north and back every day. There was no quick way to get to work, so I commuted for about an hour each day.

"You know why you were hired here, right?" said my co-worker to me the day I arrived.

"Um, why?" I asked.

"Because we're the last place station, and we're the only one that would take you," he answered.

And that described my days at that place. If I had known then what I know now about the workplace harassment laws, I would have pressed charges or at least reported the abuse. At one point, my coworkers cut the head off a picture of me and placed it on a cut-out of a model's body. It didn't do well for my struggling body image and was just plain cruel.

It was a competitive and challenging environment. I worked 80 hours per week, and it was there that I first started to realize that I had anxiety issues. My boss, who was quite nice in spite of the co-workers, pointed this out to me.

"Glori, you need to go see a doctor. It's not healthy to have that much anxiety. You know there's medication for that, don't you?" he said.

I respected him and liked his kindness, which is why I followed his advice. I went to the doctor, and it was the first time I tested out anxiety medication. The doctor prescribed Prozac, which was all the rage in the late 1990s. The meds have helped me cope at various times.

Thinking of my anxiety medically for the first time was a step in the right direction. I still had far to come on my path of healing and taking care of myself, but eventually, I stopped trying to ignore my problems.

Getting Hitched

Gary and I decided to get married. The fact that we pulled off our wedding was proof of our love for each other and of our ability and desire to get it done. Poor in cash, but rich with love, hope and promise, we didn't wait until we could do it in fairy-tale style. Our union was more important than the show of it.

With cash constraints severely limiting us, we did it on the cheap. There was no elegant wedding or fancy ring; we just wanted to get married. It was pragmatic to hold the wedding in Drayton Valley, my Aunt Fern's town, reasoning that my mom could stay with Aunt Fern—but the more important factor was that we knew it would be cheap. Event demand in Drayton Valley is never too high. The Westwynd Hotel, where we held the reception, was not fancy. No aspect of the wedding was.

I was in a hurry to get the wedding done, and we weren't about to wait for the perfect situation. I often joke that I was damaged goods and Gary was a great catch. Most brides are nervous on their wedding day, but my attitude was, "Let's get this done, let's marry him before he changes his mind!" I'm only partly joking. I was still struggling with self-worth issues at the time. Thankfully, I didn't run towards self-destructive behaviour in my relationship, and I thank God every day for Gary.

We got married with $2,000 from my tax return. Our guests ate an $11 per plate turkey dinner, we paid a photographer $300, found a good deal on a limo, I bought a dress at a garage sale for $100, and the wedding went off well.

We already knew by then that we were going to spend our lives together, but now it was official. We were together for better or for worse.

There were plenty of both to come.

Building Bridges

I didn't love the job, but several essential relationships began, and life events happened during my tenure at the radio station. I already had Gary, the most important relationship in my life, but I also met the woman who'd become my best and most loyal friend.

Her name is Ilan, and she is one of the most beautiful women I know, both inside and out. Her friendship was a blessing, and I learned so much from her. When we met, she was working as the marketing coordinator at Global TV. We crossed paths through work since we were both in broadcasting.

Many people have come into my life, and many have left, but Ilan has remained constant. Other friends have been glitzier, and at times, that perceived glamour drew me. With Ilan, there has never been any pretension or competition. She's the honest, steadfast, and true friend that everyone needs. She's always been there for me. I'm so grateful for her friendship. She's the kind of friend who isn't afraid to question me when I'm not true to myself, the type of friend I can tell my deepest fears and secrets. Her steadfast ability to see and voice the truth would eventually push me towards one of the greatest gifts I've ever received.

g[squared]

For many reasons, the radio job wasn't much better than the industrial desk. First, my salary only increased from $22,000 at the temp agency to $23,000 per year at the radio station. Second, I was working 80 hours per week. Not helpful for my anxiety and general health. Third, the commute was killing me. Add 10 hours of driving to go with the 80 hours of work per week, and I was exhausted all the time, surviving only on caffeine. Fourth, my co-workers' competitive and abusive behaviour was intolerable.

On the positive side, I was doing promotions for a radio station, which meant I was working much closer to my dream job in marketing. I had a unique opportunity. I was in contact with different companies every day, and many of them took notice that I hustled and would do whatever it took to get the job done. Many of them liked the way I worked.

I knew I just needed a start to prove I could do things on my own. I was always going to start my own business eventually. I'm just too different to fit in working for someone forever. I'm too eccentric and eclectic not to have my own business. Though I always knew I'd be an entrepreneur, I didn't expect to start my own business at the age of 23. I only needed a couple of clients to quit my gig at the radio station.

With one "big" client, Klondike Days, an annual summer festival in Edmonton, and a couple of smaller clients like Carmelo's Profumaria, I quit my job to start my marketing firm.

My income shrank to $1,500 per month but my freedom grew. Gary again played a significant role. He maintained a stable job, allowing me to take the risk of starting a business. But more importantly, he believed in the vision. Oh, and there was the little matter of coming up with the company name too. It seems like most of our memorable conversations happened while lying in bed late at night. This one happened in our new dream house, which we'd barely managed to purchase a couple of months earlier.

"I'm going to start my own marketing company," I said.

"Okay," replied Gary. He'd also known it would eventually happen. As we lay there dreaming about the beautiful future, we brainstormed some names.

"Why don't we call it g[squared]," said Gary.

The name had a great ring to it, and it left the door open for Gary to join the business once it was running and stable. With a small income and belief in spades, I left FM105 and struck out on my own for a brighter future. It's remarkable how much this episode mirrored the day my dad quit his job and started his own real estate company.

When it comes to my parents, I always saw myself more in my dad than in my mom. My mom loved and cared, my dad was smart and driven. As a 23-year-old, when it came time for me to leave the radio station and start my own business, it wasn't surprising that I did it just like my dad.

I left on a whim, without a strong plan or a stable base of clients. My only stable base was Gary, who was now working as a land negotiator for Fern's husband, Dan. I would sink or swim in business, but I knew Gary had us covered.

g[squared] was born.

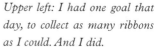

Upper left: I had one goal that day, to collect as many ribbons as I could. And I did.

Upper right: I'll always remember the joy I felt running. The secret that early morning runners don't want you to know is how beautiful and peaceful the world is at that time of day.

Left: Running was my escape. For part of my day I wasn't the angry girl who'd been abused by her step-grandfather, I was Glori, the runner who could beat anyone.

Left: Gary and I met at Dalhousie University. He is the greatest gift I've ever received.

Middle: Gary, the love of my life. We have been married 24 years and counting.

Below: As with any business, g[squared] struggled at the very beginning but it took only a couple of years for g[squared] to get up and running for real.

ALBERTA VENTURE'S TOP 30

Edmonton companies growing by leaps and bounds

Ilan is the best and most loyal friend anyone could ever ask for. Her friendship was a blessing, and I learned so much from her.

Theo is a close personal friend and one of our most powerful allies in the fight against child sexual abuse.

Eileen LaBonte started as a donor but became a second mother to me. She was a force of nature once we started renovating and moving into the Ranch.

Eileen LaBonte became a second mother to me. She believed in my heart, calling and purpose and helped my dreams come true.

Alison is the embodiment of the Little Warriors movement and one of the most courageous Little Warriors on earth. Alison raised thousands of dollars for the Ranch.

Dawn Taylor volunteered every weekend and poured her heart and soul into the renovations at the Be Brave Ranch.

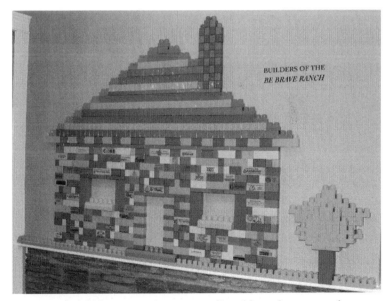

My dream would have never became a reality without the support of so many individuals and business who came together to help build the Be Brave Ranch.

Left: Chris Erickson and I at one of our Be Brave Luncheons. He was the first male to be a spokesperson in our ad campaigns.

Below: Jason Paquette showed up on the first volunteer day of the Ranch renovations and he never missed a day in the months it took to complete.

Above: The grand opening made me happy, but one of the most satisfying moments of my life came when the first of the kids arrived with their friends and family.

Right: Heather was always there when I needed her the most either as a friend or a volunteer. I could always count on her.

Right: I'm grateful to have met Kay and am inspired by her courage and the leadership she's shown. She is just another of my Little Warriors.

Middle: Hailey is one of my little angels. She's the first victor kid I ever met face to face.

Below: My dream team. Laurie, Shannon and Wanda are like sisters to me. We've been through so much together and we can't forget Rugby.

Seeing the first group of kids come to the Ranch—hugging them and eating lunch with them, just seeing them doing better after a couple of weeks—it really is honestly a dream come true.

This is the entire LaBonte family. It's through their generosity and love that the Be Brave Ranch is what it is today.

We wanted kids to have a place where they could feel special, where they could heal and form bonds with their peers. A place to know they weren't alone as victims in spite of the trauma they'd experienced.

The Little Warriors Be Brave Ranch by Ray La-Bonte and Family is a specialized, trauma-informed evidence-based, treatment centre focused on helping children who have been sexually abused, as well as their families.

I've just started to share my story and it comes from a place of love, faith and vulnerability.

I was so honoured and humbled to win the 2020 L'Oréal Paris Women of Worth Honouree Award.

CHAPTER 14

THE EGO YEARS

"When we deny our stories, they define us. When we own our stories, we get to write a brave new ending."

— *Brené Brown*

The Next Stage of Survival

The survivor has one focus—make it through one more day. My survival mode manifested in different ways throughout the different stages of my life.

During the years of my abuse, survival meant finding places to hide from my abuser. Sometimes it meant peeing my pants for fear of going into the bathroom where I'd be trapped and abused again. Survival involved creating imaginary worlds where the abuse didn't happen.

In my telling the truth and being isolated stage, survival meant hiding from others. It meant being silent. It meant waiting until I could be free and fighting the impulse to commit suicide.

As a high school student, survival meant being obsessed with competitive running. It meant finding self-worth through winning and fiercely protecting my relationships.

In university, survival meant seeking the comfort of domineering men. Somewhere deep down, I believed little old me needed protection, and I didn't know how to do it myself.

You can see how surviving can eventually become a dangerous business. Every one of those survival tactics has a downside. By basing self-worth on winning, it's hard to see much good in yourself when you lose. The so-called safety of overbearing relationships isn't so safe or healthy when your priorities are squashed or when others control your behaviour.

Still, I count myself lucky. Seeking self-worth through accomplishment is better than some of the coping mechanisms trauma survivors often use. Many seek refuge in a bottle, pills and other destructive behaviours. In the mind of the survivor, it's about hiding from the pain, if only for a short time. This unhealthy need drives decisions.

In recent years the survivor community gained a significant advocate in Theo Fleury, who shared his story of abuse and the resulting alcoholism and drug addiction he faced. Theo is a close personal friend and one of our most powerful allies in the fight against child sexual abuse.

After university, my refuge was business success, which fulfilled a deep need for my damaged ego. It made me feel important, needed and powerful. I'm not saying business was only about ego for me, but in those days it was a big piece.

As with any business, g[squared] struggled at the very beginning. Even the best company, in the hottest market, with the savviest CEO, goes through growing pains. Heck, there are ups and downs all throughout the lifetime of a business. But, starting up is the time most business leaders are filled with doubt and struggle. It takes time to build systems, grow relationships and gain expertise.

The best analogy is that of the rocket ship going to space. Ninety-five percent of the energy required by a rocket burns up in the initial push to get out of earth's atmosphere. Orbiting requires far less energy. I won't say that my business "orbit" has been smooth and straightforward, but it took only a couple of years for g[squared] to get up and running for real.

Ever since I was a young girl I've loved to solve problems. The successful solutions that g[squared] offered to businesses catapulted us to the top with an unbelievable pedigree of satisfied clients. g[squared] became a strategic communications and marketing firm, arguably one of the best in Canada. In 2020, four staff members will celebrate 10 years and one will celebrate 15 with our company. In addition, our success positioned me to be one of five women out of 140 business leaders involved with the Young Presidents' Organization in Alberta.

I've spent so much of my life feeling worthless. I still felt worthless at my core, but I discovered I was good at business. Skill and hustle are cultural gold. I had plenty of both. Success meant I would be loved and respected. The better I did in business, the more people looked up to me and respected me in a way I'd never previously experienced. My clients loved me because I helped make them lots of money. My staff needed me for paycheques and career advancement. Others showed awe and respect at the money I made.

Business success filled all the gaps in my life.

What I came to learn later was that compensating with business, shopping, alcohol, food, exercise or anything else doesn't work. You can't ignore healing. Trauma leaves a hole in your soul. The pain always shows up in some other part of life until we heal.

Leading From Fear

There were cracks in my life. I couldn't see the cracks, but that doesn't mean they weren't there. Focusing purely on business would never be enough.

The first crack showed up in my body. I didn't yet understand that my body was a barometer for whether or not I was living well. The body keeps score. When I look back at photos of myself from that time, it becomes evident that I wasn't living right. Ever since university, when I gained my "freshman 30," I struggled with my weight. I went from high-level athletic training with a lean and mean body to a sedentary university lifestyle where pizza was a diet staple.

Business success, with all the early mornings, late nights, breakfast meetings, lunch meetings and dinner meetings proved to be another health trap for me. As my business grew, my waistline grew with it. Only a couple of years into the g[squared] era, I was 50 pounds overweight.

It's bizarre to look back at photos and to think of those times because I had no awareness of my situation. I operated day to day without thought of the bigger picture, without any idea of my well-being.

Achieve. Achieve. Achieve. More. More. More. Money. Money. Money. Survive. Just survive.

Stay busy and don't look around.

Eat. Hustle. Spend. Work. Eat. Hustle. Spend. Work

The way I treated myself was one crack in the plan, but the way I treated others, especially my staff, was perhaps an even bigger crack. Poorly managed relationships are probably the only thing that deteriorates faster than poorly maintained health.

Back then, I thought of my staff as dispensable. Just as you buy something at Wal-Mart, use it, then throw it away, I acquired staff members, used them, then fired them. These were my "ego years" in business. I feel no pride in this era because of the way I treated people. Yeah, I experienced trauma, but this is no excuse for the way I treated my staff. I didn't respect them, and I was hasty to fire them. No doubt, many of my former staff members still don't respect me. I deserve this. It's my biggest regret. But it was inevitable at the time.

Everything and everyone was a tool for me to get more of what I thought I needed—more success, more food, more clothing, more for me. People were no different than a new software program or a networking event. They were all tools for my success. I've since learned I was leading out of fear. It wasn't until much later that I learned the difference between fear-based leadership and love-based leadership.

I've learned that as the leader, I can have plenty of success for myself without compromising the way I treat other human beings. My staff can succeed, feel loved, feel valued, and this does not detract from my success.

Quite the opposite—I've learned that my staff's success adds to my success. When I lead with love, we all win. Love is my mantra now, but in the ego years leading with love was a foreign idea to me.

How Marriages Fail

My unhealthy body was a symptom of my unhealthy mental state. Leading from fear was the same. However, the worst sign of my disconnectedness appeared as a crack in my relationship with Gary. To put things succinctly, there was a problem with me in our relationship. There was no problem with him, and it's to his ever-lasting credit that he stuck it out with me during the ego years. I can't say I would have been as patient with me if put in the same situation.

Gary saw something in me long before I ever saw it in myself, and perhaps that's why he was able to stick it out. I wouldn't be alive today without him. I was on a path to suicide and ruin. Gary saw me through that, and he remained by my side even when I disconnected. Not surprisingly though, our relationship was far from healthy. Ego is not a recipe for a healthy and happy marriage.

To understand how far I'd fallen off my path, you need to know my state of mind at the time.

For several years I'd been experiencing anxiety. The episode in university when I mistook a young man for Wib was an extreme example, fuelled by alcohol. Day to day, I experienced anxiety. The anxiety didn't always cause outright hallucinations, as it did that night, but fear caused delusions. It affected the way I saw myself and the way I interacted with others.

Downtime, including sleep, meant fear and anxiety. I woke up with nightmares every night for 13 years of marriage, but it was hard for me to see the proverbial forest for the trees. Anxiety, like all forms of mental illness, is challenging to comprehend for all involved—the person experiencing it and her loved ones.

Even though these things were happening to me, I didn't understand them. Externally, there was nothing wrong with me, but internally, I suffered minute by minute. I lived under the tyranny of fear and worry, and since nobody else saw it, I suffered alone.

Anxiety is kind of like the feeling Frodo experiences carrying the burden of the ring in Lord of the Rings. There is a constant dread that something horrible is going to happen in the next moment, or that you're already horrible, or that nobody likes you.

At the same time, I was a high achiever. I had business and monetary success. Others treated me with respect for the first time, as someone to be emulated. Rather than taking comfort in this, feeling better about myself and letting my anxiety diminish, I allowed the external success and admiration of others to fuel further anxiety.

Trauma survivors have a twisted inner world. External success can make internal anxiety worse, as others think we have it all together, but we know how imperfect we are inside.

I felt like a fraud.

Many abuse survivors blatantly abuse their bodies through alcoholism, drug addiction, prostitution or extreme promiscuity. Other than a couple of wild parties in university, I wasn't a big drinker. I never did drugs, nor did I sleep around. I didn't act out in many of the common ways, but I internalized everything.

My self-talk was abusive.

I always told myself I was horrible, stupid, worthless, and worse. I used my fragile psyche as the dumping grounds for my toxic feelings. For several years I didn't know what was wrong with me. Eventually, with the right help, I was diagnosed with extreme post-traumatic stress disorder and anxiety disorder.

Mental illness is real, even if many or most people don't understand it. Many of the doctors I encountered over the years assumed that since there was nothing wrong physically that my anxiety would go away at some point.

Such is the uphill battle we face with mental illness. Many doctors don't understand mental illness. Fortunately, some doctors do. The critical point most people (including doctors) miss is that the physical structure of the brain changes through abuse and other trauma. Change in brain function is one cause of mental illness.

Once the neural pathways of abuse and dysfunction set in the brain, it's not just a matter of "deciding" to change. Choosing is part of the process, but it's not immediate. It takes years of focused effort along with love, support, and at times, professional help, to heal from abuse. Rewiring the brain is a long and arduous process. It's complicated, and it often requires professional advice.

More than anything, it takes a choice to repeatedly pick yourself off the ground, dust yourself off and work on healing again and again.

Healing was nowhere on my radar during the ego years. Looking back, I'm not surprised that my relationship with Gary soured. I was deeply mired in anxiety, internal strife and self-hatred. It's no surprise I tried to sabotage the steadiest aspect of my life, my marriage.

The Joy and Pain of Motherhood

So much happened during those years. I hustled hard to gain recognition and success in business. Gary and I were still young and relatively newlyweds. I was building g[squared]. We bought a house. And we started a family.

A few years into the g[squared] era, our first daughter Rae came into the world. My pregnancy was harder than I ever imagined but when I saw Rae for the first time I fell madly in love with her. Mom was the first to visit me in the hospital. She brought me a pizza and a beautiful white dress and bonnet she had knitted for my girl. I ate the whole pizza and Rae wore the knitted outfit home.

I love my big girl. Rae couldn't have been more beautiful and vibrant. Gary and I describe her as the perfect blend of our personalities. She's a woman now, wise beyond her years, kind and loving. Her pursuit of becoming a lawyer is just one of the many reasons I'm so proud of her.

We always did our best with Rae, and there's no doubt we did many things right, but I had no idea how to care for a baby when she first came into the world.

The idea of "natural" motherhood didn't happen for me. First of all, the demands of g[squared] meant that I had to hustle to survive. There's no maternity leave for the owner of a small start-up marketing company. There's just business or no business. If I had stopped juggling for more than a couple of days, the eggs would have smashed on the floor.

I waited for three days and got back to work. I remember sitting on a cushion on my office chair, making calls, hustling, still in a lot of pain. I had to. Or at least I felt like I had to.

After work, I'd be with my baby Rae and feel like a fish out of water. I remember waiting for Gary at the front steps of our house.

When he'd come up the driveway at the end of his workday, I'd hand him Rae and plead, "help."

It wasn't all bad. I had a lot of joy with my baby, too. But that period was the unhealthiest of my life. Physically, I was eating bad food and too much of it. Emotionally I pushed everything under the surface. Spiritually, I was empty.

It's interesting looking back now because each of my four kids represents another step forward in my journey of getting well. With Rae, I was very unwell. She made me want to get well.

Much had changed five years later when I gave birth to our second daughter, Paulina. Gary and I had the parenting thing down pretty well by then. I still had my weaknesses, no doubt. But by the time Paulina arrived, I was willing to accept my parenting weaknesses. I knew I had great strengths, too. No parent is perfect. We all bring different strengths and weaknesses to the table. I was on my way to healing when Paulina was born. She's a mini version of me. Labour with her reminded me of myself—she wanted to come out and wasn't willing to wait around to do it.

When my labour started at home, I immediately got Gary to drive me to the hospital. The doctors didn't think I was in labour, but I knew I was. They sent me home, and within three hours, I was back in the hospital. My water broke, and the whole show only lasted two hours.

That's the way little Paulina lives her life too. Paulina gets it done. She excels at everything she does. And she's happy doing it. By the time we had Paulina, I was starting to see a bigger purpose for my life. I knew that I didn't want to be solely focused on work and money anymore.

Almost Throwing It Away

I didn't expect success would shut down loving my husband.

I was willing to accept some of the other symptoms of my success obsession, and for a time I entertained the idea of treating my marriage like another disposable item to be tossed aside once there was no need for it. Yes, for a moment, I thought about ending it with Gary. How did I get there?

On my ego trip, I treated Gary like a disapproving professor treats a failing student. I judged him harshly without trying to understand the whole picture.

"I'm doing all of this, and what have you done?" I thought many times.

I didn't respect his contributions to our family and our relationship. In my mind, I was successful, but he wasn't doing much. How delusional was I? I couldn't see just how much Gary had been doing. I couldn't see that everything I did would have been impossible without Gary. I couldn't have started my business or succeeded without him by my side.

I failed to see that Gary could have been equally as successful as me in business, but that he chose stability at that time, for the good of the family. When operating out of ego, we rationalize that we're responsible for everything good that happens to us, and others are responsible for everything wrong that happens.

That was me on the surface, but on a deeper level, I think I was trying to sabotage the best thing in my life. Remember how I thought Gary was such a great catch and I was damaged goods? This is how it manifested—sabotage. On the surface, it was the opposite. I was a big achiever. He was still working at a mundane, steady job, as if that's a bad thing. For the first six years of g[squared], Gary continued working as a sales manager at Corporate Express.

Gary's job wasn't as glamorous as my business, and since I identified with my work, I didn't think Gary was doing much. In my ego I thought I'd "outgrown" him. In hindsight, it was me who was missing some crucial facts. Gary's stability was one of the primary reasons I was attracted to him in the first place. Now, in my twisted state of mind, I was acting as though that was a negative thing.

While I thought everything was perfect in my business, Gary knew it was a good idea for him to keep a stable job. Start-ups are always at risk, especially in the early years. If you add my fragile mental state to the inherent risks of business ownership, it's clear that things weren't so stable in my business after all. Gary maintained our family's stability, both financially and emotionally. Things have changed now, and I've learned to respect Gary's sense of responsibility and balance genuinely.

The lowest I ever sunk during the ego years was when I briefly entertained the thought of leaving Gary. As these thoughts were rushing through my mind that day, I looked in the mirror and understood the problem.

The problem was staring back at me.

I don't remember the exact moment I came to the truth. It was probably seeing him with our daughter, who was little at the time, or perhaps it was in one of his small acts of love, like putting on the kettle for me in the morning. It's the way he loves that I love most. He's the one who brought out my ability to give love. I was deluded about our relationship; it was that love that brought me back to the truth.

The truth was a bitter pill to swallow, but it honestly did set me free. Once I saw that it was me who wasn't present, me who was creating the problems, and me who was delusional, I was able to step back in and reclaim my relationship with the man I loved. Leaning back in and investing in repairing my relationship with Gary was an early stage of my healing journey. Looking back, I think it might have been the first step I ever took on the road to true healing.

CHAPTER 15

COMING BACK TO CENTRE

"For a wound to be healed it needs to be exposed—air has to get to it—and treatment needs to be applied. All of those possibilities exist only when we acknowledge the injury."

— *Danielle Strickland*

Learning to Surrender

I wish I could say that my healing journey has been quick, efficient and problem-free.

But I can't.

There have been so many lessons—lots of them recurring. God teaches us lessons, and if we don't learn the first time, then the same experience comes back again in another way. I've thought a lot about this. Why do we not learn? Why don't we do what we know is good for us? The answer is more straightforward than you might think. We don't spend the time. We want the results of healing, but we don't invest in it as we invest in other things. Instead, we fill our time with other things. Healing gets put on the back burner. We end up needing to learn the same lessons again and again.

Regardless of these difficulties, I wouldn't change a thing about my healing path. Healing is the only path to a happy, fulfilled and peaceful life.

Sadly, many people never find the path of wellness, and I can understand why. Perhaps "path" or "journey" is the wrong word. Maybe it's more like "battle." You need to fight and scrape for every gain. I know I have had my share of struggles, and I've often used the setbacks as rocket fuel to achieve externally. Internally, though, nothing allows healing like merely letting go, not scraping and fighting.

It's as painful to examine and treat something internal as it is to clean an open wound. Still, cleaning the wound is the most critical part of the healing. Letting the wound fester leads to more significant problems down the road. With a firm commitment and a support system in place, I was able to get back up, dust myself off and continue on the healing journey every time a new challenge arose. I learned to take care of myself, listen to my body and take time for me. I started doing yoga for physical and mental health. This helped, but I still had setbacks.

Whenever a new low point came, I turned to prayer. It was through these powerful moments that I learned what surrender was, and only through surrender was I able to finally move forward.

Surrender was the most challenging lesson for me.

I've learned that we can walk the path and take the necessary actions, but it's in God's hands to bring the result. Being overly attached to the outcome of any action only leads to unhappiness and further frustration. Being proactive and taking every reasonable step to get better is essential, but there comes the point when trying to control everything, including our healing, becomes a hindrance. The ego thinks it's in control, but it's not. God is in control. All we can do is take the proper steps. The outcome will be what it will be.

Surrendering the outcome starts the healing.

I've proven this lesson over and over. Every time I surrender, something better comes along. Looking honestly at my relationship with Gary and admitting I was the problem forced me to surrender.

In the depths of the ego years, I wanted Gary to fit my idea of what he should be. I was trying to control the outcome of his actions. When I couldn't remake him into what I thought he should be, I started blaming him rather than accepting my responsibility in the matter. My ego thought it knew better than God what I needed in a husband.

Letting go of that attachment was an early lesson in surrender. Once I started accepting Gary for himself and realized there was a good reason for everything, our relationship improved immediately. Ironically, once I let go, my dream scenario unfolded. Gary joined g[squared]—on his own accord. Of course, I was thrilled about this. The company now officially had both G's at the forefront. We were united as a family in love and also in business.

With this first big moment of surrender, some of my most significant personal changes came. By starting to heal me, I began finding the strength to help others. This process is what taught me that to be in the service of others and make a difference in the world, we must first heal ourselves.

As with so many moments in my relationship with Gary, our relationship healing was a watershed. A crack of light started shining inside me the moment I surrendered. I started acting from love, and within a couple of years, the significant changes began to come.

The Quest for Robert

As the healing light entered and my life started changing, Gary and I began thinking about more kids. By this time we were beginning to think globally.

We researched the need for orphan care and adoption that so many countries have. The year was 2005, and there were many celebrities bringing attention to the issue through their adoptions and actions. The need was becoming well known, and we began to think seriously about the idea of adopting our next baby from beyond Canada's borders.

After much research, we became enamoured with Ethiopia. There was a significant need, and as we learned more about the country, we knew we wanted to adopt a baby from Ethiopia. When I think of the millions of babies in the world needing care and love, it makes my heart so sad. The basic premise of living a life of love and being a warrior means I have to do something about it.

Why not live for love with family, too? Every baby brought into the world deserves love and respect. Sadly, there are plenty of birth parents who can't provide that.

We wanted to expand our family and adopting a baby made so much sense. We started the adoption process in 2005, and it took over two years to finally "give birth" to our baby. Little Robert was born in the summer of 2007. Gary and I were working at g[squared] one day in December when we received an email from the adoption agency. There was a picture of our baby boy. Our hearts melted on the spot, and we wanted to get him immediately.

But international adoptions must go through the proper channels. Bureaucracy moves slowly, and we were forced to wait as the wheels spun. It pained us to wait six months before we could get him. Finally, in the late spring of 2008, Gary and I went to Ethiopia to pick him up. That trip changed our life dramatically, as we were able to do some humanitarian work in addition to picking up our baby. We've since been back a few times and will return in the future.

At last, the day came when we could go see Robert at the orphanage. The policy is to come one day and see your new baby then return the next day to take him home. I'm not entirely sure why they do this, but after holding him and seeing him in person, we couldn't possibly go another night without him.

Babies begin to develop attachment immediately when they are born. They need to feel the safety and comfort of a parent. The nurses in orphanages do the best they can. But just by sheer volume, they can't hold every baby as much as the baby needs.

GLORI MELDRUM

When we first saw Robert, he didn't react well. He was limp and wouldn't come to us. He didn't respond to anything. He'd been through so much loss already, and if babies aren't able to attach to a caregiver from birth, they don't develop as well.

I knew we needed to be with him immediately. We came all this way to adopt him. I couldn't allow us to abandon him even if just for the night. I started pushing to bring our baby home that day. For the rest of the day, Gary and I took turns holding and getting to know Robert and negotiating with the orphanage people.

It was funny because there was another couple there adopting a baby of their own, and they loved Gary and me because they saw what we were doing and they knew it meant they could get their baby the same day, too.

Slowly over the day, Robert warmed up to us and eventually, we won our argument with the orphanage. We jumped on a rickety old bus holding Robert and headed back to our hotel. I'll never forget dinner that night. From being completely disinterested when we first saw him that day, he had already started to come around by night. I played peekaboo, and he played with Gary's watch. I knew he'd be just fine. He just needed love, as we all do.

The next morning at breakfast he was eating eggs off of our plate, and I knew the bonding had begun in earnest. Since then, Robert has grown into such a sweet, loving young boy. He loves to cuddle and is an absolute lady-killer. He's so handsome and strong and is just a wonderful addition to our family.

A Powerful Vision

Significant external changes started happening a few years after making internal changes. I always preach that everything good in life begins from self-improvement.

So, it's no surprise a significant turning point in my life happened in the year 2005, not long after I'd dedicated myself to healing. I attended the Entrepreneur Organization (EO) conference in Montreal, Quebec. Imagine that room for a moment—500 entrepreneurs sitting around tables listening to speakers in entrepreneurship, networking and forging relationships.

Including myself, there might have been 50 women in the entire crowd. Yes, business is still mostly an old boys club, but I've never been one to pay attention to those unwritten rules. Many important changes happened in and out of the room that weekend, especially for me. They had nothing to do with business, though.

The night before the conference started, I attended what's known as an EO "dine around." Small groups of entrepreneurs eat together at a restaurant, trade ideas and network. Eleven of us attended that night. We walked in, sat down and immediately my eyes shot to the wall across from our table where I saw the most incredible piece of native art—a stylized warrior—similar in style to many other paintings but somehow unlike any I'd seen before. It's hard to describe the feeling this painting stirred in me, a feeling below conscious thought. I transfixed on it.

The warrior held a shield in one hand as he raised a bow above his head with the other. The strength he exuded didn't come from his weapons, but rather the proud, ready-for-anything stance with which he faced his unseen enemy.

It's not as though I was an art connoisseur, coolly assessing the work's values and flaws. I didn't even like native art before that night. The painting plus being with this group of dynamic and successful entrepreneurs created an intoxicating combination. For the first time in several years, I found myself tipping back more than my maximum of two glasses of wine.

One thing was clear—I wanted that painting. I wanted it right then and there, so I started negotiating on the price. I approached the woman who was in charge of selling the art, and she told me an intriguing story about the artist who created the painting. I have to give her credit. She was using what I thought was a solid sales technique. She explained how the painter lives on a sailboat in the Caribbean. Every few months he comes to port, sends the paintings off to his dealer, and then goes back out on the boat where he creates more paintings.

I negotiated for the painting most of the night. She insisted it wasn't for sale. I raised my offer to $5,000 at one point. I would have done anything to get this painting. It consumed me, but I had my limitations. Five thousand dollars was exponentially more than I had ever paid for a piece of art, and I couldn't go any higher. Only when she firmly told me it wasn't for sale at any price, I finally conceded that I wouldn't be able to own it.

The painting was out of my reach, but not out of my mind. When I returned to the hotel, Gary was waiting. He had accompanied me to Montreal, so we could make a holiday out of the trip once the conference was over. I was no sooner through the hotel room door, that I launched into the story of the painting, how much I wanted it and what I offered for it. He responded in a measured tone, "Well, it's a good thing you didn't get it; that's a lot of money."

I knew he made sense and would soon recognize that it wasn't so much the physical painting but what it represented to me. This truth clicked as I fell asleep. All these years, I had imagined myself as a warrior against the world, fighting a lonely battle against the darkness that surrounded me. The painting symbolized me taking up a warrior stance for real—not in a childish, defensive way, but in the form of a mature, confident adult. I had transitioned from a warrior fighting for survival to a warrior of healing.

My subconscious had awoken me to my mission, I hauled myself out of bed the next morning in time for the first conference session.

Eight o'clock.

Usually, I'm a sleep-in kind of gal, not one to wake up early to attend an early morning workshop session without having a strong reason.

This session didn't mean much to me.

It was an award ceremony dedicated to a businessman named David Ash, the founder of a hugely successful payday loan company. On this day he received an award for his philanthropic efforts helping Vancouver's homeless.

Mr. Ash told the story of his mother, Vivian Grace Ash, whose own mother was a sex worker. Vivian was born with syphilis and raised in foster homes, where she suffered sexual and physical abuse. Eventually, she landed in the right foster home. The family loved her, and in spite of mighty struggles, she persevered. Vivian was married, had three children and worked as a nurse's aid. She never healed, though, and mental illness caught up with her.

She spiralled downward. Drug addiction and mental health issues resulted in homelessness and struggle, and she eventually died on the streets she called home. To honour her and to do something about the problem, Mr. Ash donated $1.2 million to found the Vivian Shelter, dedicated to housing women in need.

Everything crystallized in one moment—an epiphany.

For the six months prior, I searched high and low across the country to find an organization in Canada dedicated to fighting child sexual abuse. I planned to dedicate my time, money, and resources to help such an organization. As I searched, I learned about an epidemic.

Sexual abusers only got minor sentences. On the rare occasion when a victim laid charges, the perpetrators didn't often get punished. When they are convicted, the sentencing is light beyond belief. Rarely is a sexual predator of children incarcerated longer than six months.

I learned how badly survivors have it.

During my healing process, I wanted to start doing something about the problem. I tried to help, but no organization with a comprehensive plan for assisting the victims existed. That moment it finally made sense. It was me who needed to do this. I had to lead the charge.

I felt weightless, as though I was about to float out of my seat. An avalanche of ideas followed. Without thought, I reached into my bag and pulled out a pen. I grabbed some of the Fairmont hotel stationary on the table and started writing.

The only way I can describe what I experienced at that moment is that it all came through me, not by me. It occurred to me that my life had been building up to this moment. All the time and hard work I had put into creating my business gave me the knowledge I needed to set up the structure my new organization would require to thrive and be successful.

The business I had chosen—advertising and marketing—gave me the skills and tools I needed to get my message out. I couldn't have planned it better if I tried.

My pen flew across the pages of my journal and only stopped when I realized that the organization would need a name. My mind flashed to the painting in the restaurant from the night before—the name came to me.

Little Warriors.

Telling Ilan

I knew from that moment my world would never be the same again. With those words, I officially declared war on child sexual abuse. As the founder of Little Warriors, I would be responsible for preparing adults and children for this war and provide them with the tools and weapons we would need to be victorious.

My mind swirled and planned over the following days, telling Gary all about my plans as we toured around Montreal. Upon arriving home, I called my great friend, Ilan, to set up a coffee date. She knew about my abuse and always supported me, so she was the first one who came to mind. On the phone, I blurted out my vision and the plans I had for Little Warriors. As always, she was there to speak the truth.

"So, when are you pressing charges, Glori?" Ilan asked.

"What do you mean?" I replied.

"You can't lead other survivors to fight sexual abuse unless you face your own. It would be hypocritical," she said.

She was right. Dammit.

I avoided this process for a long time, but now I had to press charges against my abuser officially.

Questions flooded my mind. Had too much time passed since the crime? Would it devastate my family all over again? Might I finally receive the justice I always deserved? Could Wib still kill my family?

I was scared, but the time had come.

Pressing Charges

From when I first spoke to Ilan and realized that I'd have to press charges, my mind went into overdrive. It was all-consuming, yet I struggled to face it.

I had to do it, but I couldn't do it.

I couldn't sleep. I struggled to do anything. There was no way I was going backward. Defeating child sexual abuse was now my life's mission, and I knew I needed to press charges to achieve my purpose.

Still, I avoided it—until I didn't.

Courage hit and I immediately drove to the Sherwood Park RCMP station.

I pressed charges and started Little Warriors when my eldest daughter, Rae, was eight, the same age I was when the abuse started.

I remember looking at my little angel and thinking, "What could she possibly do to deserve that?"

Nothing.

I knew this now, but somewhere in the depths of my psyche, I still felt responsible for everything that happened to me. I was the "slut," the "whore" and the "liar."

Consciously, I knew this was all untrue. I knew I'd done nothing wrong, but subconsciously I believed the horrible things they said even after all those years. We need to fight because the pain doesn't end for the abused, until long after the abuse is over. With my still-fragile psyche, I felt overwhelming fear as I entered the RCMP station to press charges.

Intellectually, I knew Wib couldn't hurt me. I was physically safe and had people to protect me no matter what happened. Then why did my body shake? Could his threat to kill my mom and sister still be affecting me?

What if he did the same to Gary, Rae, Robert and Paulina? Again, I knew it couldn't happen, but the mere thought of it was enough to make me second-guess myself as I told the officer at the desk that I was there to press charges.

Even more significant was the fear they would doubt me. It's shocking how many people out there, including some in law enforcement, don't believe the victims of child sexual abuse. They think survivors are "just making a big deal out of nothing." They tell us to "get over it," as if shaking off this crime is the psychological equivalent of a stubbed toe.

It shouldn't take much imagination to empathize with someone victimized as a child. The sad fact is many people don't have such empathy.

Unfortunately, these people are often found in the worst possible places of responsibility, like the social services lady my mom took me to see many years earlier. That was my only contact with "the system" when it came to my abuse, and I still had much fear about what it would be like to go forward.

I had no idea how the Sherwood Park RCMP would react when I told them I wanted to report a twenty-year-old crime committed by an old man on the other side of the country.

I knew how important it was, but would they?

"I'd like to press charges for sexual assault," I told the receptionist at the front desk.

"Ok, did this just happen?" she asked.

"No, it happened from when I was eight until I was 10," I replied.

"Oh."

It was like that moment on every cop show when the battle-weary cop looks incredulously at some clueless individual who's not making their life any easier. The ordeal went downhill from there. It's a cold and uncaring system. As I was half-expecting, the RCMP officer was less than excited to open an old, sexual abuse investigation.

Still, she went through the motions.

I've since learned that the correct process is to take a written statement, an audio account and a video statement at the same time. But, due to the ineptitude of a green constable on duty, I had to return to the RCMP station three separate times to make my statements.

The RCMP treated me like a nuisance at best and a suspect at worst. They put me in a cold little room to wait, and wait, and wait, before questioning me as though it was I, not Wib, who committed the crime.

The process was slow, mishandled, awkward and unhelpful. But in spite of all of that, Wib would be charged within two weeks.

Re-victimization

Pressing charges was a pain. I felt like the victim again. It was poorly handled, but I had to move on quickly and brace myself for a worse ordeal—telling my family. It meant opening myself up to relive the accusations, insults and rage.

For years I practiced the combined arts of shutting my mouth and avoiding family whenever possible. It worked. I avoided much pain, but I also knew I didn't want to end up like Vivian Ash, suffering silently and letting mental illness overcome me. It would have ultimately led to me ending my own life. It was time to speak up in spite of the inevitable pain and further alienation.

My first call went out to Aunt Fern, whom I still thought of as my protector from that scary night when she saved Bobbie and me from my mom's deranged boyfriend. When we lived in Vancouver as kids, she was like a second mother to me.

Our relationship had plenty of ups and downs over the years. She was the kindest to me throughout everything, but even her support disappeared when I needed it most.

I'll always be grateful for the times she loved and protected me. I credit her with helping Gary and I move to Edmonton, and the day in the kitchen when my whole family yelled at me and called me a slut, she showed the most support.

Still, I don't think she ever "forgave" me for the turmoil she perceived my accusations created for the family. She reacted in a way you often see in families affected by child sexual abuse. People would rather stay silent and not rock the boat rather than let justice prevail.

It's not that they don't believe the victim was abused. They think the victim is selfish by refusing to keep their trauma to themselves. It's so hard for victims to identify their molesters publicly. There are people close to them who believe it's in everyone's best interest to stay quiet.

I know first-hand how well that works. The forced silence leads the victim to feel shameful when it should be the perpetrator of the crime who feels shame.

The phone call with Fern didn't last long. I told her I'd pressed charges against her stepfather, and she expressed sadness and regret that I had done so. I asked her if I could expect her support if the case ever went to trial.

She told me she wouldn't get involved.

Part of me wished that she would have a change of heart and support me in my time of need, as she had in Vancouver. The support didn't come. Her illusion of a perfect family was in jeopardy.

I wasn't any more optimistic about the outcome of my second call, but it was the most important one I'd have to make. You see, I never believed I was Wib's only victim. Child molesters don't operate that way. I knew another girl who was close to my age and stayed with him often. She refused to confront him because she still depended on him for her day-to-day survival. In my perfect scenario, she would hear about me pressing charges, get courage and join in my fight to convict Wib of his crimes. In my heart, I knew this was unlikely.

Still, I had to try.

I called her mother.

"Hello?" she answered after a few rings.

I took a deep breath.

"It's Glori. How are things?"

"Fine."

"How's the weather out there?"

"It's been raining."

"Oh…that's too bad."

"Did you call to ask about the weather, Glori?"

"No."

"I didn't think so. What's going on?"

"I've decided to press charges against Wib."

"Of course you did. Why now? Why after all this time?"

"Because it's the right thing to do. He must be held accountable for what he did to me," I paused and allowed myself another breath before I added, "and your daughter."

"Don't bring her into this."

"You and I both know…"

"We don't know anything. She says Wib never touched her. Why shouldn't we believe her?"

"Because maybe it's in her self-interest to want to protect the man who helps keep her from living on the street?"

"You pretend to care, Glori, but when was the last time you even saw her?"

I tried to answer, but she interrupted me before I could.

"This has nothing to do with her. It's all about you. It's always about you. You want to be the one who saves her, but she doesn't want to be saved. She doesn't need to be saved."

I desperately wanted, needed their support.

"This isn't about me. It's about him. It's about what he did to us. You can deny it all you want, but we both know the terrible, unspeakable things he did. You're the one who's willing to let him get away with it just because it's convenient. Well, it may be easier to let him go unpunished, but it isn't right. I have to do what's right. What kind of example would I be setting for my children if I taught them not to fight for themselves, to just let others walk all over you because it might upset them if you fight back? What he did was wrong, and the world has to know that he did it. You could help."

"That just isn't going to happen."

"I'm sorry to hear that."

"Goodbye, Glori."

I'd always had my suspicions that Wib had abused others. In total, I named three women. Of the three I pointed out to Detective Gillespie, only one person refused to cooperate. The others added their allegations to the charges against him.

Waiting and Learning

There are few things in this world as fundamentally inhumane as bureaucracy. It turns humans into numbers and our emotions into a nuisance. I've often wondered if humanity is even possible in an administration. As victims, we're only capable of seeing our experience as personal and unique. We alone truly understand the suffering and pain.

But we represent mere numbers to many of the men and women who work our cases. They hear the same story many times. Under these circumstances, even the best of us can become jaded and cynical. It's a safety mechanism. If they suffered every victim's pain, they couldn't manage day-to-day.

The system has to change.

I don't have all of the answers, but I know someone has to start loving and caring for the victims because the cynicism of those in the system often ends up re-victimizing those with the guts to step forward. If victims weren't traumatized to begin with, they quickly become so the moment they run into the cold, uncaring and often unbelieving system.

I laid charges as an adult, but I can barely imagine what it might be like to experience the system as a child. My brief introduction to the social services lady as a kid provided a cold reminder of how often sexual abuse victims aren't believed and how often we're treated like criminals.

With the stress of the pressing charges, my anxiety ramped up again. It felt like the earth quaked every time I took a step. I ended up needing more anti-depressants. I hated relying on the chemical help, but I didn't quite have the tools to make it on my own. It took me several more years before I would accept that it's okay to take prescribed medication for anxiety.

I waited. And waited. My anxiety grew and grew. All kinds of thoughts flooded my mind. I imagined how the investigation would unfold and how the police would now go digging into every dark corner of Miramichi. What would Wib or the rest of the family do? What would they say to my mom, my sister and my dad?

I waited to hear about my case. Anxiety deepened. Weeks passed and I heard nothing. Soon, it began to feel like I didn't exist to the police. I heard nothing.

There was a good reason for this—I followed up on my case only to find out the police in Miramichi didn't even know I existed. Over a month after I laid charges against Wib, they had yet to receive the file. I felt anxiety for nothing. A month of hell passed, and the investigation hadn't even started.

I found out the Sherwood Park RCMP lost my file.

Unbelievable.

All my fear, struggle, and a lifetime of anxiety, lost in bureaucratic limbo. Not one to let things sit, I took matters into my own hands and called the RCMP every single day. Each day they told me the same thing, "We're doing everything possible to find your missing case file. We'll send it to Miramichi once we find it."

Right.

I didn't see it at the time, but in many ways it was a blessing, as was every step of my crooked and steep path. I needed to have total empathy with survivors, so I needed to experience every type of setback.

The experience provided the perfect opportunity for two things. First, I would have to learn how to surrender. I needed to be able to let go of the notion that I could control everything. It was up to God, as he had a plan for me. In this case, God planned to make me wait for an excruciating month. I didn't understand surrender then. The RCMP fiasco was just the first step that slowly taught me to surrender.

Second, it taught me how to take the experiences every survivor goes through and turn them into rocket fuel. It's a pretty simple analogy that I originally got from my dad. Rocket fuel makes things go faster and stronger. I have been using rocket fuel my whole life, but now I needed the cleanest, purest rocket fuel to make a real difference for child sexual abuse survivors.

On the one hand, you need to practice surrender by letting go of the need to control everything that's going on. On the other hand, you need to take action, do things, make phone calls and do whatever it takes to make a change.

I slowly learned that I couldn't wait for the government, the bureaucracy or any other system to make real change in the realm of child sexual abuse. It's not surprising if you think about it—the system allowed things to get where they are. Why would this system be the one to change it?

Real change can only come from the people, from dedicated individuals. I learned that we would have to create a movement so loud they couldn't ignore it.

I waited some more.

CHAPTER 16

THE TRIAL OF MY TRIAL

"Trial, temptations, disappointments—all these are helps instead of hindrances if one uses them rightly. They not only test the fiber of character but also strengthen it. Every trial endured and weathered in the right spirit makes a soul nobler and stronger than it was before."

— *James Buckham Kennedy*

Waiting for Nothing

The waiting killed me. As an entrepreneur, I have at least some measure of control over my destiny.

Surrender means letting go of the outcome, not the process. We still control our actions, but with my case, I was truly helpless. There was no way into the bureaucratic mess. Other than the daily phone calls, I was powerless. I had no political cards to play.

I've treated most aspects of my life as a business problem to be solved. Take the right actions and eventually, the results come. In university, when I wanted Gary in my study group, I asked him to join. When I want a business contract, I ask the potential client for the deal. But when it came time to convict my abuser, I felt utterly powerless. There was nothing that I could do to unlock the bureaucratic mess.

I didn't like feeling powerless.

Time kept ticking.

An entire year passed before my file was finally tracked down and charges were laid against Wib. It was a classic case of legal limbo, which nobody should be forced to endure.

The Investigation Finally Begins

The Canadian judicial system is inhumane, ineffective and slow. The system is made up of people, and some are great people. In my case, I want to recognize one incredible man who genuinely cared and tried with every ounce of his being to make a difference. His name is Dewey Gillespie, the detective in Miramichi who took on my file.

Detective Gillespie did an exemplary job, which shocked me a bit after the delays in the case. He taught me that every individual could make a difference. It's called "actually caring," and is a remarkable thing. Once the file landed on his desk, he took on the case with all his heart. I immediately received a call from him for an interview. I was off to New Brunswick for the first interview of the investigation.

The most pertinent question Detective Gillespie asked was if I could think of anyone else Wib might have molested. I shared some names and he followed up with each one. His interview techniques must have been effective because the other girls came forward with their stories, adding their allegations to the charges against him. Dewey Gillespie is a real detective, in it for the right reasons. He's compassionate and committed to justice. He cared for the other victims and me. He believed us. His interest was to bring a criminal to justice. To him, we were people, not just another file. He treated us with dignity.

I can't stress enough how important it was having Detective Gillespie believe us. Survivors become accustomed to being disbelieved. It's a sad state of affairs. Whenever I think of this fact, it makes me question the world we live in and realize how precious empathy is. False sexual abuse allegations are shockingly rare, as nobody wants to be associated with sexual abuse due to the stigma. The real problem is the opposite, getting victims to come forward. Right now, there are millions of people suffering silently because of their fear of speaking out. The cost to public health is enormous.

What would happen if we all acted out of love as Detective Gillespie did, rather than self-interest or cold detachment? The world would be a much better place. Epidemics like child sexual abuse would end.

I can't say enough good things about him, and my hope is that the whole world can take a turn in his direction. I was comfortable telling him everything that might help him, and when he asked me about other potential victims, I was happy to share my thoughts.

A Case of Stockholm Syndrome

The girl who refused to co-operate is a couple of years older than me, and, like me, had spent a lot of time with Wib. She confided in me once, a long time ago, but now denies it. Strangely, it was she who brought up the topic to me several years ago.

I'll never forget it.

It was clear something was on her mind when we got together, and I soon found out she wanted to discuss Wib's abuse.

"I know what Wib did to you, Glori," she said.

"Oh, really?" I replied.

"Yes, he did the same thing to me," she said.

"Um, okay," I said. I was many years away from understanding my feelings about the matter or knowing what to do about it.

"But I'm not going to do anything about it."

At that point, I wasn't planning on doing anything about it either.

Abuse affects everyone in different ways. I was determined to prove the voices in my head wrong and prove my worth to the world through achievement. The other girl stayed in a childlike state, needing help to survive—even to this day. Wib himself provided her with financial support. The trade-off for his "kindness" was silence.

She played along with the silence game, and suffered the brutal inner torment that goes with it.

We're not in touch anymore, so I don't know her current circumstance.

Still, it's not hard to guess.

Staying in the Hole

Over the years I've seen enough survivors to know that the other girl is a classic case of a survivor choosing to "stay in the hole"—a term I started using to describe survivors who for whatever reason can't see far enough to make a change. I've been there, and I get it, so I'm not judging. I'm just sad about it. I've met hundreds of survivors. Some take control of their lives and their long path to healing, and some choose to remain in the hole.

The hole is self-loathing and self-abuse. The hole is deep, dark and lonely. It's a place where victims continue to self-abuse long after the physical acts of abuse have stopped.

I've met enough survivors now to recognize that I can't get down into the hole with anyone. I can love and support them, but I can't go down in the hole. I can throw them a rope, but it's up to them to use the rope to climb out.

I'm not suggesting every survivor who hasn't pressed charges is choosing the hole. Deciding to press charges or not is deeply personal for survivors. I don't judge any survivor about his or her decisions. But a survivor who continues to remain under the influence of his or her abuser stays in the abuse long after the abuse is over.

Stockholm syndrome is when a victim empathizes and identifies with the abuser. True love can't exist between an abuser and a victim.

A Sort of Redemption

Three women, two others and me alleged sexual abuse against Wib. This corroboration was redemption for me.

I wasn't sure if there would ever be justice in the courts, but it was sadly comforting to know that the other girls corroborated my story. Deep down, I still believed that the corroboration of others would bring my family to my side. Alas, it was never about belief. It was about power and willful ignorance. My family knew what was going on, but they chose to silence me and pretend it never happened. The corroboration didn't change a thing in my family, but I felt vindicated when other women came forward.

I wasn't alone.

My vindication came at a price. The two girls who testified about Wib's sexual abuse meant Wib had abused girls in addition to me. I hurt for them. Serial child molesters abuse on average 100 children, which means he may have had many more victims.

Serial child molesters are physically attracted to children. The desire is stronger than their ability to control, which is why there is no cure for them. Child molesters must be identified and taken away from children immediately and forever. It's the only way to stop them from victimizing more children.

Sadly, there would never be any real justice for Wib. It was too little, too late.

The Pre-trial

With three accusers in place, the case was set to go to pre-trial, but first I had the pleasure of meeting the crown prosecutor—what a joy.

If you're unfamiliar with the court system in Canada, you might be thinking, "Why were you only meeting your lawyer this late?" That would be a good question if the crown prosecutor were my lawyer. In our system, the accused hires his or her lawyer, but the accuser is stuck with the crown prosecutor.

Early on, I mistakenly believed the crown prosecutor was my lawyer. He quickly cured me of that belief when I met him. One of the first things he said to me was, "I'm representing the Queen and country, Glori. I'm not your lawyer."

"So, who is my lawyer?" I asked.

"Nobody," he replied.

It might seem like semantics to some, but it's a meaningful difference when it's your case and real justice is on the line. I would never have hired this particular lawyer. If I had the choice, I would've employed a lawyer whose interests were more aligned with my own. I would have hired a lawyer who was as passionate about ending child sexual abuse as I was.

I would have gotten a butt-kicker.

Instead, I got the crown prosecutor.

I'm sure there's some reason why the system works this way, but it seemed so dehumanizing. Wib didn't molest the Queen or the country. He did molest the other girls and me. Couldn't we choose our representation? How do we even know if the crown prosecutor cares about putting sexual predators in jail? There are still many uneducated assumptions in the world, and as unbelievable as it might seem, some people don't consider it a serious crime. Often they think people are laying charges because an uncle or grandfather "tapped them on the ass on the way up the stairs." Victims are horrifically abused and remain silent for life.

The boy or girl who cries wolf about child sexual abuse is rare. There are two reasons for this.

First, unless exposed to it, kids have no frame of reference to level such allegations. They can't usually imagine it and have no reason to fake it.

Second, as adults, most people know the attention garnered from accusations of sexual abuse is far worse for the accuser than the perpetrator. The number of victims who never lay charges is proof of how intense the social pressure against victims can be.

I never had the confidence that the crown prosecutor assigned to my case was passionate about convicting Wib. His immediate "setting me straight" about his role as protector of Queen and country set the bar low, but having no other choice, we went forward.

To be clear, I can't complain about the crown prosecutor's procedural rigor. Even though I didn't believe his convictions were as strong as mine, I know he went through the correct procedures, including preparing me to take the stand.

The day before the preliminary trial, we held a "practice session" privately in his office. His questioning was so severe it induced panic in me. I hyperventilated so bad that at one point, the prosecutor nearly had his assistant call an ambulance. Recalling the abuse is a significant trigger. Doing it under pressure makes it even worse. Before this episode, I checked into the hospital several times for panic attacks. It didn't bode well for the next day when I'd have to take the stand and answer the same questions.

Forming a Sisterhood

Being face to face with one's abuser is horrifying under any circumstance. I did it plenty of times, and it never got more comfortable.

I remember the terror of sitting beside Wib in church. I remember the terror of being forced to sit on his lap for bizarre versions of "let's pretend this didn't happen." I remember being handed the phone on Christmas morning to find Wib on the other end. I did everything I could to avoid him for years, and I froze with terror each time I had to face him. I didn't know what to do or say, and after each encounter I suffered severe anxiety.

Over the years I distanced myself from the entire family (especially Wib). I hadn't seen or heard from them in almost 20 years. I just had to face him one more time. One last time on a cold, miserable morning inside the courthouse in Miramichi.

Small towns can be comforting and homey, but I have mostly painful memories of my small town. Visiting Miramichi at any time is like going back to prison for me. The claustrophobic sensation of being there only grew the day of my pre-trial.

The courthouse in Miramichi is a tiny, old box of a building. There is nowhere to run or hide. Sitting in the lobby before the start of court, I peeked out the window. I froze in place as Wib walked up the stairs. Not that this should have surprised me. I was there to charge him with a crime, and the provincial courts summoned him. He had to be there. In spite of all that, this man still triggered horror in me.

Looking out the window at him, I saw that he also brought my grandmother, great aunt (my grandmother's sister) and my great aunt's husband. Later, I found out that Uncle Cam and his wife also came to support Wib. These were the most vicious of his supporters, so again I shouldn't have been surprised. They reminded me of a family mafia. It was this crew of six that terrorized me the most as a child after I went public with the abuse. They were still playing their power game.

Back during the kitchen meeting discussing my allegations, it was Cam and his wife who were the most vicious calling me a whore, a bitch and a slut. Twenty years later and my testimony to all the horrible things Wib had done to me didn't change a thing. Wib never testified on his own behalf that he did not do them, and after he pleaded guilty to fondling two other children who testified during that same pre-trial, nothing changed in the way I was treated by my family. They still supported the convicted child molester over me. I'd be lying if I said this didn't hurt. The difference now is that rather than spur more self-loathing inside of me, there is an opportunity to reflect on how lost and alone I imagine they must be. Instead of having the guts to do the right thing and acknowledge my suffering could have happened, even in some small way, they continue to profess the criminal's innocence.

Rather than believing her granddaughter, my grandmother stayed with my abuser despite hearing everything that he had done to me. I imagine that she must have been scared and alone in the world if she thought she needed this man. Learning empathy and seeing through eyes of love taught me this.

On my day in court, though, I went into panic mode at seeing them all. In addition to facing my abuser, I also had to face the family again. My poor mother was caught between supporting me and her ties to family. As much as she believed me, I asked her to remain home so she wouldn't have to choose sides.

The moments before pre-trial brought one gift. I finally got to talk to the two other girls who'd also come forward. It was sad because we were all there for the same horrific reason, but it was great to be in this together. It was comforting to know I had some sisters with a common interest who supported me, if only from a silent distance. I felt a bit of pride, too. I was the one to first press charges and brought the matter to court. Without me coming forward, these women might never have had their day in court.

This day proved, if only on a small scale, that one person's courage could be enough to elevate others' courage to stand up and fight against their abuser. Survivors and advocates can make a difference in the lives of other survivors through support, and through setting the example of courage.

Of the three of us, I had the strongest case against Wib. He committed worse abuse against me than he did the other girls. With them, he must not have had as much time alone because he'd "only" fondled them compared to the things he did to me. Still, we were sisters who'd survived the devastation of abuse at the hands of Wib. He was our common enemy, and we were all in court for justice.

My Day in Court

It felt so crowded in the tiny courtroom. I was a few feet away from Wib, and soon I would have to do the most courageous thing I'd ever done. My grandmother sat in the back row of the spectators' benches, knitting from the moment she sat down until the end of the pre-trial. I guess the rhythmic tapping of the knitting needles soothed her. She didn't seem too perturbed by anything.

I already felt claustrophobic and panicky. My breathing was shallow, which worried me. I hyperventilated other times in the past from panic attacks, and I could sense a vicious panic attack coming on even before being called to the stand.

The judge, defense lawyer and crown prosecutor underwent their formal discussions before getting started. My memories of that entire procedure are blurred together. It was happening somewhere else.

My moment of truth came quickly.

"I call Glori Meldrum," the crown prosecutor said.

I felt panicky before that, but pure terror hit me for real when I was called into the courtroom. I made it through the doors but that was all my body would allow. The fear grabbed hold of my body, and my feet sunk into two feet of quickly drying concrete. I couldn't move.

I've since learned about strange, out-of-body experiences where people experience a distorted version of time. I know what they mean because I stood there frozen for what felt like hours, as the entire courtroom stared. Only Detective Gillespie recognized something was wrong.

"Glori, are you OK?" he shouted as he jumped out of his seat.

I couldn't even answer him. Everything stopped. I could only perceive my twisted version of reality at that moment. I had no power to move or act. With my body incapacitated, I came close to fainting. Fearing I would lose this moment and that Wib would win, I did as I'd been doing my entire life.

"God, please get me through this. I beg you." I spoke inside my head.

This mini moment of surrender worked. In a heartbeat, I started to relax. Beginning from my shoulders and moving down my body to my feet, the tension disappeared. My feet released from the imaginary concrete, and I walked towards the stand. As I moved forward, I felt God gently place his hands on my shoulders.

I can't explain in words the power of that moment. It was one of those few occasions when a crack opened up and light flooded in. I can't logically explain this phenomenon, but each time I've had this feeling of light coming through cracks, it's enabled me to see clearly, live more happily, or do something I otherwise couldn't do. In this case, I consider it a miracle because I couldn't even face Wib or think about him without experiencing horror and panic. Once the crack opened up, I could do it.

Much like the day I scribbled out the Little Warriors vision, this happened through me, not by me. I had no control, merely acting as a conduit instead.

I took the stand and testified for two hours without breaking. I told the details of the abuse. I shared how Wib threatened to kill my mom and sister if I ever came forward. I testified about the psychological damage the abuse had on me for years afterward. I did it all with strength, not a scared child or even a survivor, but as a proud warrior.

Post Pre-trial Debriefing

Each testimony was offered individually. Afterwards, the three accusers had a meeting with the crown prosecutor. The purpose of the meeting was to debrief us on the potential for our trial going forward, and I learned that a pre-trial is no guarantee of an actual trial.

After the meeting between all four of us, the crown prosecutor pulled me aside for a separate meeting, where he started talking about an ongoing Supreme Court case. It was called R. v. Trochym, and the crown prosecutor told me the result of this case would set a precedent for those cases where witnesses experienced hypnosis. That case was relevant to mine because I went under hypnotism at the age of 14.

I sat in utter disbelief as the crown prosecutor explained R. v. Trochym to me. Depending on how the ruling went, my testimony might not be admissible in court.

My case was stayed and the outcome now rested solely on the testimony of the other two women.

Emotion flooded over me. Why? Why now? No doubt thousands of people had undergone hypnotism in the past, and their testimony was allowed. Couldn't this happen 10 years later? R. v.

Trochym wasn't settled, and I already had a sinking feeling that Wib wouldn't see justice for the crimes he committed against me.

Waiting Again

Months had passed since the pre-trial, and I didn't hear anything.

In the meantime, R. v. Trochym came to its inevitable conclusion. The Supreme Court ruled that testimony from witnesses who underwent hypnosis wasn't allowed in a trial. The ruling nullified anything I had to say in the eyes of the court. No other witnesses could attest to the things Wib did to me, and the case was effectively lost.

Silenced again—this time by the system that was supposed to protect me.

The Supreme Court of Canada creates laws of the highest legal authority in our country. Those rulings set judicial precedent. Overturning legal precedent and setting a new one is extremely difficult. There was no way a lowly court in Miramichi would ever attempt to overturn the legal precedent set in R. vs. Trochym.

Eight months after the pre-trial, I received a phone call from Detective Gillespie. He cried as he explained why the case was dropped. He faxed over the entire ten-page legal opinion from the crown prosecutor explaining why the crown would not be pursuing the charges I levelled against Wib.

Of course, it was the hypnosis. There were no credible records of what I'd said under hypnosis, and in any case, it didn't matter since testimony from people who'd been hypnotized was now inadmissible.

A Return to Anxiety

I received Detective Gillespie's call while driving with my friend and colleague Freeda.

My hope for justice died, and within moments of hanging up the phone, I was inconsolable. We were on our way to close a business deal, but my sobbing put an end to that plan. Freeda had no choice but to drive me back to the office. She called to cancel our meeting, drove back to the office, helped me out of the car, and again I was paralyzed, this time by grief.

I collapsed onto the parking lot of g[squared], sobbing, and hyperventilating. Again it was a blur that I can't remember well. All I know is that the intense grief and anxiety scared the entire staff half to death. Gary was out of the office at the time, so one of the team members called him to pick me up. He came, but nothing could help at that moment. I was devastated.

Wib would never serve a day for the crimes he committed against me. All was lost. Gary gathered me up and took me home where I stayed in bed with nothing but grief for a few days. I didn't know if the fight would ever come back. Eventually, it returned, and the first thing I did was call the crown prosecutor.

"I want you to talk to the press about this. This ruling is wrong. We need to get the word out." I said.

"I told you before Glori. I'm not your lawyer. I represent the crown," he replied.

"You're a coward. You don't even care about justice," I said.

Ultimately, the crown prosecutor believed the case wasn't worth pursuing. Now he was telling me he wouldn't do anything about the travesty of justice that had just happened.

Another blow.

Of course, I wish I had a better experience with the legal system. I wanted my abuser jailed for the things he did to me. I wish the crown prosecutor cared. I hoped for many different things that never happened, but I also know that all of it happened for a reason. By the time my case was abandoned, I'd experienced the full spectrum of re-victimization.

Ilan was so right when she first urged me to charge Wib, not just to avoid being a hypocrite, but also to put me through the experience of re-victimization. Without experiencing this, I could never fight against child sexual abuse with the same strength.

The End is a Beginning

I got angry after my sobbing died down. Still seeking some form of justice, I called my grandmother. Wib answered.

"Put her on the phone!" I screamed.

Surprisingly, he obeyed. In a moment, my grandmother was on the phone. "You always knew what he was doing to us!" I cried.

"You were always a liar, Glori," she responded

"You should be ashamed. You go to bed at night and wake up in the morning next to a child molester," I said.

The conversation didn't go on long before she hung up. But I gathered in our brief exchange that nobody told them my case got stayed. Being the first to tell them gave me no comfort. The only bright spot in this whole mess, other than the lessons learned, came from the ongoing case. The court removed my accusations, but the other girls' accusations stayed. The court eventually convicted Wib on lesser charges of fondling the other two girls, and in the end, he received two years of community service.

Still, he received nothing for my abuse. I knew what it felt like to be denied justice in the courts, and with R. v. Trochym setting precedent in the Supreme Court of Canada, thousands of other abuse survivors will never get justice in our court system either.

Hypnosis was a standard method of "extracting" the truth in decades past. That nullified the testimony of thousands of men and women. Starting with the abuse itself, then being silenced by the family, and then receiving cold and uncaring treatment from the Sherwood Park RCMP, to finally being let down by the justice system—I experienced the whole range of survivor hell.

God wanted me to know every level at which victims of sexual abuse suffer. The job was now complete. I could officially take a leadership role in the fight against child sexual abuse.

But, before my mission began, there was still more work to be done in me.

CHAPTER 17

HITTING ROCK BOTTOM

"To forgive is to set a prisoner free and discover that
the prisoner was you."

— *Lewis B. Smedes*

Losing Faith

The outcome of the pre-trial devastated me. The concept of surrender had not yet sunk into my psyche. In truth, I didn't have a clue about surrender, only the beginnings of a fuzzy understanding.

Most of the time, I still believed that I could control every situation. I took a bad result as a personal failure and sign that everything was wrong. Only in hindsight can I see that I had to go through the tribulations of suffering to grow. I was not so noble at the time.

The legal fiasco crushed me, and I went into a deep depression again. I hit rock bottom while driving back to Edmonton from our lake property. Gary and I took two separate vehicles to the lake that weekend. After a distracted weekend where my mind was all over the place, we headed home. I was in my car, driving alone, and the kids were with Gary following me.

I felt alone, like a fraud and a failure.

More accurately, I knew I was alone. I knew I was a fraud and a failure.

Such is the mindset of a depressed person. I wanted it to be over. I was sick of fighting, sick of battling, sick of the endless struggle to feel good. The abuse felt like an ongoing event. The sickness crushed me. At that moment, I thought seriously about ending my life. All I would have to do is jerk the car into the ditch.

I understand a suicide attempt. Some people call it a "cry for help," but that's BS. Many people have a moment similar to mine, where they come close but never tell anyone. It's not a cry for help. It's rock bottom.

If you've ever read my good friend Theo Fleury's book, you'll recognize that he had his rock bottom suicide attempt. I can't say I was reckless, like Theo, in the same way. I didn't do drugs or drink, but I see the survivor's grasping in both of our actions, and I understand what it's like to come close.

I don't know what stopped me from swerving off the road in that instant, but do know I was close. A moment later, gratitude overcame me. My kids followed behind only a couple hundred yards. My loving husband drove them. I loved them, didn't I?

"What is wrong with me?" I thought.

Something needed to change. I knew it in that moment it was not the outside world. I mean, sure, it had to change there. That's what the vision for Little Warriors was about, but something needed to change within me more. On this path, I might make a massive impact on child sexual abuse, but it would kill me in the process.

"I thought I had it all figured out," I told myself.

Working on the external was no longer enough. It was time to tackle the demons within. Work, money, possessions and even battling child sexual abuse didn't change the internal. Charging Wib didn't heal me. And as much I wanted it otherwise, a full victory in court wouldn't have healed me either. It couldn't have healed me.

I wanted to stop child sexual abuse. I wanted it bad, but that day as I drove home from the lake, I had not yet begun true healing for myself. I made positive strides, such as accepting full responsibility in my relationship with Gary, but I hadn't experienced true healing yet.

Fighting to change laws and prevent further abuse could never make me whole. Moreover, Little Warriors needed a leader who had experienced healing to help other survivors. Something needed to change. And it had to be within me. It was time to learn why I felt the way I did. It was time to understand why nothing I did could give me lasting peace.

I needed to get better, for my kids, for Gary, for Little Warriors.

And for me.

The Path to True Healing

I became a seeker of truth. Not the truth of some esoteric tradition, or even the commonly held realities of our society. I began seeking my truth.

For decades now, I believed I could "get over this thing." If only I could achieve a bit more, or I could figure it out and be better by changing the external reality of child sexual abuse through Little Warriors. There were even times when I thought I could get over it by just shutting my mouth and pretending everything was OK.

Throughout it all, there were a few constants. I felt unhappy, unhealthy and broken. Nothing internal worked. I'd done so much in my life. Looking at myself through someone else's eyes, I had it all. Shouldn't I be happy and healthy too?

Pondering death woke me up. I needed help. My prescription meds helped me manage anxiety, but I wanted to go a step further. I wanted wholeness, so I finally surrendered my control and reached out for help through a program of therapy called the Hoffman Process.

The Hoffman Process is a unique, eight-day intensive residential program. It's a deep dive into the first 12 years of your childhood to see how and why you may have become like your parents and how these patterns of behaviour may not be serving you well in your personal and professional life today. The Hoffman Process provides emotional tools to help a participant let go of limiting belief systems so they can enjoy the banquet of life instead of just settling for crumbs.

The Hoffman Process focuses on childhood trauma. I knew most of my psychological issues stemmed from my early childhood, the abuse and the lack of stable parenting. I knew exploring my childhood would be crucial, but I had no idea how important. Professional guidance from the Hoffman Process made all the difference.

There is a Hoffman Process local to Alberta but I wanted to go far away due to my public profile in Edmonton through g[squared] and Little Warriors. I didn't have celebrity status by any means, but enough people knew me that I figured the chances were too high that I'd be recognized. I didn't want people finding out that the Little Warriors lady didn't have her stuff together, so I chose to do the Hoffman Process at the Toronto location.

Part of the Hoffman Process is disconnecting from regular life. Once inside, participants can't use cell phones or have any contact with the outside world, barring an emergency. The process is all about getting in touch with what's inside and understanding the pain. It's about releasing the pain and freeing oneself of the past.

Let's face it, for "busyness" junkies like myself at the time, getting away from all the pressures of life was vital. I needed this space.

We use so many things to distract us. We have TV, cell phones, friends, shopping, restaurants and work, anything to avoid facing the pain inside. Distractions make us feel OK for a time. But when we're alone with our thoughts, when we turn off the cell phone, when we turn off the TV, then how do we feel? That's the question everyone needs to ask. The Hoffman Process and inner healing aren't just for survivors. They're for everyone.

I firmly believe this is the key to a better world—a massive shift towards self-improvement and inner healing. As a society, we focus entirely on external circumstances, but we mostly ignore internal healing. The ability to act with love is the fundamental building block of a better world. Can you love yourself? If you can't, it's impossible to work with respect for others. Inner healing is the doorway to self-love.

People often think caring for oneself before others is selfish. The opposite is true. We can't genuinely care for others until we can care for ourselves. It might seem counterintuitive, but caring for oneself is an unselfish act because it frees us to truly serve others, which explains why we have such a massive lack of compassion in our world. Not many people know how to love themselves. It's an epidemic. There is no other way to explain how lost people are.

Think of it this way. Why aren't giving and working for the betterment of the world our most common activities? It's not like we can't do these things. We live in a time of unparalleled wealth. Many of us have normalized things like trips to Vegas, owning a new car for each adult in the house, owning a big home for that matter, shopping at designer stores, and buying lattes at Starbucks.

What's the point of all the work our society has done in the past centuries? Did we amass this wealth to continue wasting it on needless things? We're rich in money but poor in spirit, and the debt in our society proves this. We make so much money, yet so many struggle to make monthly payments. We always feel we don't have enough, so we consume more and more.

Keeping up with the Joneses would be a thing of the past if we were more concerned with love and our internal well-being than with consumption and appearance. Despite our ego's false belief, money is not our biggest concern. We make money the essential thing, inviting greed and lack into our lives. However, nothing is lacking in our real lives. The only thing lacking is the strength of spirit.

In this land of material wealth, there's a poverty of spirit and a lack of well-being. So many feel unhappy and tormented, yet they continue to focus on money, possessions and consumption rather than real prosperity through personal growth. We can't imagine spending our free time and money helping others because we see ourselves as lacking. Our distractions, too, come from this lack of well-being.

The Hoffman Process forces participants to abandon distractions. Trust me, when you're a serial busybody it can be challenging to be alone.

I did it anyways.

So there I was, out in a forest retreat with nothing but a bunch of other seekers and a couple of facilitators.

But my ego wasn't going to give in without a fight.

Delving Into the Process

Everyone engaged with the expressed purpose of dealing with pain. Participants had experienced everything from severe abuse, to people who were pressured by their parents, to people who'd discovered a dead parent.

I learned something important: The level of pain people experience isn't correlated with the severity of their trauma. Even seemingly small experiences can stick with a person and retain hold over them for years.

Everybody needs to understand this point. The pain and struggle we experience aren't necessarily about the severity of trauma. It's about what the trauma means to each person. Our inner child doesn't necessarily distinguish between different levels of injury.

Doing this kind of deep psychological work, getting in touch with the inner child, is easier said than done. I knew I had to do something, but doing it is a struggle. My ego wasn't about to let go of me quickly. Ego clung to me like a cat on the edge of a ten-story building.

The facilitators did everything they could to help us grow and understand ourselves. Some of the participants understood it right away, but my ego put up a mighty struggle.

"I'm wealthy, I have a great marriage, I've got everything figured out," I contended. There was a niggling little voice in my head.

"Why are you here then, Glori?" it said.

The battle between my ego and my desire to change continued for some time. Ego would block me from learning the lessons. Courage would push me closer. Ego would pull me away again, and courage would bring me back. My ego wanted me to believe the external success meant I was okay, but I knew this was a lie. It was painful, but I stayed and eventually started to get it.

Seeing the Truth

The turning point for me came during an exercise involving a bat and a pillow. Yes, a bat and a pillow. Just as a child punches a pillow when angry, we were taught to take our anger out on a pillow. The exercise wasn't just for venting, though. The purpose was to get us in touch with our real feelings. Many of us carry anger without being genuinely aware of the hold it has over us. We think anger toward others proves something to them, but in truth, it only affects us.

The facilitators coached us to wail on the pillow and let our anger boil to the surface. I half-heartedly hit the pillow while people all around me were pouring all of their hate and violence into their pillows. Keep in mind this exercise was four days into the experience. The process was half over, and I hadn't even begun to explore my hurt. I hadn't even started to see the truth of my pain.

"Come on Glori, hit the pillow harder, let your anger out," the facilitator urged me on.

Yawn. "I have my stuff figured out," I thought silently.

"Let out all your anger," she implored.

To get her out of my face, I began hitting the pillow harder, but the motion of swinging harder did something. My pure anger released. Another "crack" opened, like the one I experienced in the Mirimachi courtroom. Without realizing it, I slammed my bat into the pillow harder and harder. Sweating and screaming now, I hit the pillow until a thought slammed into my mind, "I hate myself!"

And it was true.

When truth speaks, you cannot ignore it. I found my truth, not some piece of obscure knowledge gleaned from an outside source and half-heartedly applied to my circumstances. Nobody could have made me believe it, but I could see it and feel it for the first time.

It screamed. It screamed so loud there could be no doubt about its truth. It screamed so loud that it roared out of my mouth.

"I hate myself!"

Not Wib. Not my family. Not a business enemy. Not even sexual predators. I hated myself. Tears came. I fell into a heap. I sobbed and sobbed and sobbed for what felt like hours.

Me. The golden child. The successful businesswoman. The doer. The founder of Little Warriors. The boss. The wife. The mother. I was the person who had it all figured out, but I'd blocked myself from understanding this self-hatred for so very long. I'd used money, success, materialism, consumption, distraction, shopping and more to prevent this feeling. But the belief was relentless. It kept returning. It was this belief that drove me to the thought of suicide.

Truth. Sweet truth. Now I knew it.

I hated myself and had for a long time.

Moving Forward With Truth

A truth once grasped can only be ignored at your peril.

Just as the truth sets you free, ignoring the truth keeps you shackled in a private prison of your own making. I can't say where I'd be today if I'd ignored the reality of my self-hatred. Once I grasped it, I wanted to live up to my truth, so I decided to make the most of the Hoffman Process. I had four days left.

As I'd done so many times before with business goals, I now committed the full force of my energy to the inner journey. While the emotional journey is somewhat more elusive, I knew that I could make progress by applying myself. It was time to tackle my self-hatred. I needed to get in touch with the causes of the self-hatred. We were instructed to write, "hate" letters, which we would later burn, to all of the people who wronged us. I didn't want to burn mine as I was still attached to blaming others, but I did the exercise anyways and felt an enormous release of blame.

I wrote about all of the different ways I was wronged and why I was angry with the people involved.

To my mom: I wrote how I was angry about being exposed to violent men when I was a child. I wrote of my anger at being left in Wib's hands and the lack of protection and safety I felt.

To my dad: I wrote of my feelings of being abandoned by him. I wrote of the distance he kept from us.

To Wib: I wrote of the abuse and why I hated him for abusing me.

Even though none of them saw the letters, the process worked. The power of it doesn't come from the other people reading the letter. The power is in the process of writing. Getting one's feelings and emotions onto paper is freeing. The ritual of burning the letter is a tangible way to let go of attachment. By physically letting go of the words, I emotionally let go of them, too.

Then the facilitator explained the next step of the process, "Okay Glori, now it's time to forgive Wib."

The notion of forgiving the monster seemed ridiculous. Why would I ever do that? My anger and hatred towards him gave me strength, motivation and power. Or, so I thought.

On reflection, my anger towards him weakened me. Consider this: I did the Hoffman Process approximately 25 years after the abuse had ended. I held onto pain and hatred the entire time. These toxic emotions ate at me for decades. Meanwhile, Wib was feeling none of the pain. If he had any regrets or bad feelings, it wasn't because of my anger.

We falsely believe that in letting go of anger we're "letting them off the hook." In truth, we're only letting ourselves off the hook by releasing our forgiveness. So, who was benefiting from my hatred and violence? I certainly wasn't, and he wasn't being punished by it. Forgiveness isn't for the perpetrator; it's for the victim. It's to free oneself from the pain of past hurt, and with the facilitator's guidance, I eventually chose to forgive Wib.

"He never has to know you've forgiven him, Glori," she reassured me.

I went ahead with what she taught me. I had to use Wib's story as a gateway to forgiveness. By empathizing with his story, it would become apparent that he only did his best. He deserved forgiveness. I knew my parents' stories. I knew why they'd inadvertently hurt me. However, I knew nothing of his story. All I could think was how horrible he was. I only knew the monster. How could I forgive this monster?

"If you don't know his real story, then you need to make up a story as to why he is the way he is," she said.

Following the facilitator's lead, I invented a story about how he was sexually abused. I created an account that he'd experienced even more pain than I had, and that he had no way of healing and that as a result, he re-enacted the pain by abusing others. I made up the story that it was only pure chance that I happened to be the one who crossed his path. I even expressed some gratitude for the fact that I was called to make a difference in child sexual abuse. The abuse I suffered ended up serving a higher purpose for the world.

A person can forgive in their heart but still do the right thing in the external world. I forgave Wib and knew he was only acting from his own messed up state, but I always knew he should be charged, prosecuted and convicted for his crime.

I can forgive, knowing that every person, even my abuser, has a story. Some are incapable of doing the right thing, but I can continue to do the right thing to ensure abuse stops. Forgiveness is an internal process. In the outer world, I still held Wib accountable for his crimes.

This piece evades so many survivors. Forgiveness is not for the abuser; it's for the abused. My family members told me that I must forgive so many times, but you can't force a survivor to forgive. Forced forgiveness doesn't work. It must come from within, and its only purpose is to bring peace to the person who forgives.

The purpose of this book is to demonstrate healing. I want people to heal. It's not about continuing to wallow in the pain of the abuse. It's about dealing with the damage, growing from it and eventually freeing oneself from it.

I'm not trying to force anyone to forgive, but I genuinely hope others can see my example and learn from it. I was in a personal hell for decades before allowing myself to forgive Wib. All I can do is show other survivors that forgiveness will bring them more peace. To become a victor over sexual abuse and move on from being a victim, survivors must forgive. It's an essential step.

The proof showed up in my life immediately. My nightmares stopped as soon as I forgave Wib; that very night I had my first nightmare-free sleep in decades.

Forgiveness releases the forgiver.

Creating the Future in My Mind

Forgiveness followed awareness, but the Hoffman Process by no means ended there. We moved onto exercises that showed me I could create my future through my thoughts.

Attending my funeral changed my life. Okay, it was a bit creepy to be lying on a plastic bag on the forest floor in sub-zero winter temperatures—disturbing but compelling. I was instructed to attend two different funerals.

"If you were to die today, how would you die?" the facilitator asked me.

That was an easy question. I thought seriously about it a few months earlier. "I would run my car off the road. Suicide," I replied.

The facilitator told me to go out to the forest and lay down, imagining I was in the ground, buried at my funeral. An eerie, but powerful, energy engulfed me, as I imagined each of my loved ones walking up to my body and leaving me a message.

"You always wanted one person to love you, and I gave you that. You're the love of my life. I'm going to miss you," said Gary to me as I lay in the imaginary coffin.

"Thanks a lot, you're not going to see me grow up, go to university, or have my kids. You were a selfish bitch," I imagined my oldest daughter Rae (a teenager) to say.

"All I ever wanted was a mommy," said my little girl, Paulina.

"I thought you wanted to be with me," said Robert.

Next, my Little Warriors spoke.

"If you can't do it, we can't do it either," they said.

Bawling, I got up off the forest floor and walked back to my room to sleep. The experience left me completely drained. I slept like the dead, but I woke with a bolstered resolve to heal myself. I knew that the path I was on before would lead me to the fate I'd imagined during my funeral. I knew I had to heal from within so I could avoid the horrible future I'd imagined. I had to heal me, love me, and strengthen me so that I could be there for the others.

My goals hadn't changed, but the difference was I understood the critical piece to achieve these goals was my well-being. The next day I was to attend my funeral again but under drastically different circumstances

"Imagine yourself years down the road, but this time you've lived the life of your dreams. What will the same people say about you at your funeral now?" the facilitator asked.

I went off to the forest with my plastic bag, and once more I lay on the forest floor, getting into my imaginary coffin.

"I love you," said Gary.

"Thank you for showing us the way. Thank you for being there. We're strong, happy, and fulfilled women thanks to you," said Rae and Paulina.

"Thank you Mom for rescuing me," said Robert.

"Thank you, Glori. Together we've healed millions of survivors. Together we changed the laws and sentencing for sex offenders," said my fellow Little Warriors.

I got up from my coffin and walked back to my room, but this time, I didn't walk back to the room. I floated—energized by the possibility of the future. We're going to die anyways, why not make our death what we want it to be? My resolve to heal grew to levels I couldn't previously imagine.

Walking away from the experience, I knew the second funeral was possible. But to get there, I'd need to continue healing. I'd need to keep getting better.

True Change Comes from Within

I can't believe how much I've changed when I look back at photos of my most disconnected and unhappy days and compare them to what I see in the mirror now. By looking only at the external, you would notice that I've lost a lot of weight since those "ego years." What you wouldn't know is the spiritual reason behind it.

People now comment that I glow. Back in the ego years, I scowled. Yes, I lost weight, but the spiritual side of myself is the main reason for my change in appearance. The Hoffman Process catalyzed my efforts and made me whole. It helped bring back a part of me that had long been absent, since that day so long ago when, as a young child, I sat on the bathroom floor at my dad's house with a razor in my hand, contemplating ending my life.

I had to make a choice that day.

I didn't commit suicide. Instead, I chose to survive. I don't regret the choice I made. I had to do it to survive. I was in an early phase on the long road to healing. The decision was to silence Little Glori, to put her away. I stopped being Little Glori that day and transformed into Big Glori.

As I worked through the Hoffman Process, I realized that I hated Little Glori. Wib abused my body. The abuse itself was bad enough, but the impact on my soul was worse. I started to think of myself as dirty. When I came out with the truth, my family called me a slut and a whore. I was outcast and hated for speaking up. Although it wasn't right and there was nothing wrong with me, I internalized Wib's abuse and my family's hateful words. I believed for a very long time that I was dirty, that I was a piece of crap.

Out of sheer survival, I had to send Little Glori away and become Big Glori. Little Glori couldn't handle the painful world she found herself in. Little Glori would have killed herself that moment on my father's bathroom floor or soon after that. She had to go. I sent her away, and I became Big Glori all the time. Big Glori could keep herself alive—could survive—but Big Glori had her problems. She didn't know joy or happiness. Big Glori struggled with love.

I wasn't whole without Little Glori. The inner child is real, a component of ourselves we need to be complete. We need our inner child to feel joy, happiness and love. Silencing the inner child results in a loveless life and a miserable existence. Looking at my worst photos from the "ego years," I see a person devoid of an inner child. Silencing the inner child brings about the kind of problems I've struggled with at various times in my life.

It was a near suicide that silenced Little Glori for so long, and it was another near suicide that pushed me toward the Hoffman Process, where I invited Little Glori back into my life. I did an exercise where I spoke to Little Glori, where I told her why I'd sent her away. I had the opportunity to say I was sorry and invite her back into my life.

When you see my photos from the disconnected "ego years" and you see me now, the most significant difference is the reunification of Little Glori and Big Glori.

The Hoffman Process changed my life. I wasn't done growing and healing, but the Hoffman Process accelerated my growth and process of becoming whole. Before going I told Gary that I would come back a different person. True to my word I did.

The change happened in a way I couldn't have predicted, but it happened nonetheless.

CHAPTER 18

CREATE A MOVEMENT SO STRONG

"There is nothing as sweet as a comeback, when you are down and out, about to lose, and out of time."

— Anne Lamott

Creating a Movement

It's one thing to discover your life's purpose—it's another to take a risk and really do something about it.

Since day one in 2005, I knew Little Warriors would have to become a movement so strong we couldn't be ignored. I had no idea the risks I would need to take for Little Warriors to be successful but I was ready to do whatever it took. I channeled a passion driven by my experience to put the conversation about child sexual abuse on the map.

Search the phrase "treatment centre for kids who were sexually abused." You'll discover what I knew in 2005.

There are no treatment centres in Canada or the world to address what is the most widespread and devastating trauma today. Experts estimate one in three girls and one in six boys are sexually abused and 25 percent of human trafficking victims are children in Canada. Statistics Canada reported a 233 percent jump in child pornography incidents in the last decade. The exact number is hard to determine because many cases are not reported to authorities. A recent study by researchers at the University of

Alberta found that more than 95 percent of child sexual abuse cases are never reported to authorities.

There is little evidence that one-on-one therapies have successful outcomes for kids who were sexually abused. That's because they don't get to the root of being violated. Kids were not learning from each other in one-on-one therapy. Hearing from other abused kids would help them know they weren't alone.

I wasn't going to let the story rest there.

From as far back as I can remember, my dad always told me that I could accomplish anything I wanted. As many close friends, casual acquaintances and the odd passer-by can attest, my dad's endearingly unfiltered. He prefers to "tell it like it is"—no embellishments, insincerities or even sugar coating on his cereal. So while other kids might shrug off encouragement from their parents, I believed my dad when he told me that I could accomplish anything. I absorbed that advice and made it my truth. It gave me the courage and confidence to take risks, embrace challenges and own who I am and what I want to achieve.

So if a treatment centre was going to be built for kids, who better to spearhead it than a survivor of child sexual abuse?

In 2008 Little Warriors formalized the foundational elements of our mission:

1. Raise awareness and provide information about child sexual abuse. Scientists know that child sexual abuse can disrupt developing brain architecture. Toxic stress can lead to lifelong difficulties in learning, memory and self-regulation. Children who are exposed to serious early stress develop an exaggerated stress response that, over time, weakens their defense system against diseases, from heart disease to diabetes and depression. When we don't attend to these important aspects of development promptly, there can be serious consequences later.

2. Advocate to ensure the rights, needs and interests of children are respected and protected.

When we invest in systems to ensure all people are able to get the treatment they need, we will have a healthier and stronger society.

3. Provide child sexual abuse prevention strategies to adults through education.

Trying to change behaviour or build new skills on a foundation of brain circuits that were not wired properly when they were first formed requires more work and can be problematic. This is why Little Warriors works tirelessly to educate adults on how to help prevent child sexual abuse.

4. Build a world-class treatment facility to help children heal from the devastating effects of child sexual abuse.

The Be Brave Ranch would provide evidence-based, trauma treatment to help children who have experienced child sexual abuse, to help reduce the risk for later physical and mental health problems.

Transformative Help

Talk to any Little Warriors staff member and you come away with two insights: Each one is a standout in his or her profession and they say I inspire them.

Laurie Szymanski was hired as the Executive Director of Little Warriors in 2010. I had to kiss a lot of frogs before Laurie came to us. When I interviewed her, I fell in love with her humility and believed that God sent her to us. She is one of the most beautiful human beings in the world. Never one for the limelight, Laurie's selfless devotion is the bedrock of Little Warriors.

Shannon Phelan is typical of our employees. Shannon started with Little Warriors in 2010 as well, overseeing communications and fund development. She effuses a contagious passion for the cause. A realtor who volunteered for Little Warriors referred her to an opportunity for employment with our organization. When Shannon was hired she felt appreciated by being able to work from home and contribute as a team member in advancing vital research. She is a workhorse, doing the job of five people.

Shannon uses "us" and "we" in describing the Ranch. "I love to see how much we've grown. The work is super fast-paced, there's never a day when I'm bored, and that makes it fun. Our Research and Clinical Oversight committee is made up of leading professionals from across the country." Shannon also oversees the Prevent It training. Each year 4,500 people are trained across Canada to be aware of the signs and prevent abuse.

Laurie and Shannon are like sisters to me. We've been through so much together and we would take a bullet for each other.

Nowhere to Go

Child sexual abuse survivors experience an enormous amount of shame. The abuse can lead survivors to a higher than average use of drugs, alcohol, prostitution and involvement in the criminal justice system.

In 2011, I met a young teen who was being sexually abused and was living with her offender. We met at a Ricky's Grill in Edmonton. We hugged and I told her how brave she was and that she was loved. She wanted to know if there was somewhere she could go to get help. I told her I hadn't built the Be Brave Ranch yet, but when it was ready I would have a place for her.

I'll never forget the call informing me she had taken her own life. Her death broke me. There was so much of me that felt guilty. Although I work really hard, when she asked where she could go to get better, I felt like I wasn't doing enough, fast enough.

Unexpected Opposition

When I started poking around provincial government providers and asking questions about innovations in treatment, I should have been prepared for the responses but I didn't see them coming. No one ever came out and said, "you don't know anything" or "you don't belong here" but the icy reactions I got made it clear I was stepping on protected turf.

They were right. I don't know my way around clinical treatment but I know what it's like to be that child who has been sexually abused. I never had any resources as a kid, so what I wanted to give these kids was the ability to get better quicker and to grow up into healthy adults and not have to deal with all of the awful mental health issues that I had to deal with.

And I knew on so many levels that helping other survivors was why I was still on earth. Why I didn't kill myself on that bathroom floor. Why I didn't drive my car off the road and end it all.

What I am good at is bringing people together and being laser-focused on an outcome. I am a builder. So I went searching for an ally. We needed a respected professional who would make a good pioneer.

Dr. Peter Silverstone

"You wouldn't believe how many people I see in my clinical practice, pretty much every day, who years, or decades later are still dealing with the consequences of child sexual abuse. It's really very tragic." Those were some of the first words I heard from Dr. Peter Silverstone.

Dr. Silverstone is Professor of Psychiatry with the University of Alberta's Faculty of Medicine and Dentistry. We met while serving on the board of the Edmonton Economic Development Corporation and became instant friends. When he heard my vision for the Be Brave Ranch we became allies and he readily accepted my invitation to serve on the Board of Little Warriors.

"I'm all in Glori. Let's go."

Dr. Silverstone and I were familiar with treatments that were offered during weekly or biweekly meetings over a prolonged period. So much more was needed. We envisioned a new approach—something innovative and effective.

A Dream So Big

I wanted to build something for child sexual abuse survivors that had never been done before. What I envisioned wouldn't be a small, office-sized clinic for counselling, but a ranch-sized centre where survivors could come and live and heal. My dream was on the scale of a world-class facility, like a Mayo Clinic or a Betty Ford Centre, offering an intensive, dedicated, affordable and multi-modal treatment. We would need an unbelievable team and a partnership with a reputable research institution like the University of Alberta. And in my heart there was never a doubt that we could do this.

There is nothing tougher to market than helping child sexual abuse survivors. We got little traction with business owners or philanthropists, because they didn't want to talk about the subject. At the outset, I believed people would step up and give, but that never happened. The child sexual abuse sector wouldn't give us the time of day. Right from the start, people reminded me that I had no status in the medical community. I wasn't a psychologist, or psychiatrist or a sociologist. The non-profit sector felt threatened by me. I had never heard so many "no's" in my life. Time after time, I was told I would never pull this off.

There was nothing easy about the dream of the Be Brave Ranch. The whole journey felt like pushing the biggest boulder you could ever imagine up a massive hill. According to the naysayers the dream was impossible, so I might as well give up and stop wasting everyone's time. But, I've never been a quitter and I wasn't about to become one.

I stuck to the dream because it wasn't just my dream. I knew this was my calling. If it weren't, I would've run away a million times.

A Movement So Loud

The government of Alberta could have funded a long-term care facility like the Be Brave Ranch without needing to spend extra tax dollars. Three provincially funded "rehabilitation" facilities are in the Edmonton area for the perpetrators of child sexual abuse. There has never been a study that proves perpetrators are curable. We know survivors can get better through support, counsel, and therapy, but there is no cure for the monsters that do the crimes.

A workable solution would have been to pull some of the funding from rehabilitating the perpetrators and spending it on helping the survivors. The Ranch needed a couple million dollars—less than is spent annually in Alberta on perpetrator rehabilitation.

And it wouldn't take much to muster up the love to provide the necessary funds. I'm convinced that if any politician would sit and reflect on how horrendous child sexual abuse is he or she would become a change maker.

Try it yourself—take 10 minutes to imagine abuse happening to your son or daughter. Then imagine the emotional abuse the children suffer at the hands of their abuser. These beautiful little angels live in a state of horror for the entire period of the abuse. It's horrific to think about, but people need to think about it to prod them to take the right action. We're all capable of experiencing love. A simple meditation on the pain that children experience should be enough to make us do the right thing.

We received the opposite of love from the Government of Alberta as we tried to gather the money to build the Ranch.

We struggled and fought to get the Ranch built, pushing forward for years, and receiving Be Brave Ranch donations in small sums. Little kids donated their piggy banks, held lemonade stands, and people chipped in 50 or 100 bucks where they could. To get anything significant done in this world requires people—lots of people—working passionately in the same direction.

In the small Southern Alberta town of Coaldale, one of the most courageous Little Warriors on earth, a teenage girl named Alison, was raising thousands of dollars for the Ranch. Alison is the embodiment of the Little Warriors movement. As I would learn, the only way to make the Ranch happen would be to create a movement so loud we couldn't be ignored.

The government of Alberta did everything in its power to ignore us. Fortunately, there are good people in Canada, willing to give their time and money to do what's right. I used Facebook to share my story and the vulnerability inspired other survivors to share their story. We began to build our tribe and give a voice to survivors across the country.

It took several years, but we finally got our first couple of million in donations. Our community was pretty much tapped. We would need the big dollars to fill the gaps for operational money after building the Ranch.

I wasn't afraid to ask Edmonton's captains of industry for money. Still, I heard "no" hundreds of times. Bart Yachimec stands out above the rest because of the way he said no. He always let me down so sweetly that I returned year after year to ask him for money. Finally, in late 2012 he said yes! His company, the Yachimec Group, which owns several Edmonton auto dealerships, donated $450,000. It was our first significant money.

A Blessing In Disguise

One event above all the others taught me not to rely on the government. Again, it looked like a curse when it happened, but in hindsight, I know it was a blessing.

In early 2012 Little Warriors completed an application for government funding. It was this money that I was counting on to put us over the top, or at the very least get us close in our efforts to get the Ranch built. The $750,000 applied for would have gone a long way and undoubtedly would have been a fantastic community-building project for the government. To us, it looked like a no-brainer. We followed the proper process, filling out all the paperwork, submitting plans, budgets and projections. My government contacts left me with the impression our application was going to be approved. At last, we were going to catch a break.

When I opened the government's letter, I collapsed on the floor in tears. Our application was denied. For days, I shook with anger. At first, the stated reason for denying funding was the province didn't have money and then it was we needed to fill out more paperwork, but we learned later, there was more to the story.

So, I sat and stewed. Do we continue to go the government route knowing that it would take months if not years before our funding request ever got through committees and perhaps a new bill? I decided to share the letter with Theo Fleury. Theo had the highest profile of any Canadian in the fight against child sexual abuse.

Theo published the letter on a Thursday, and the media storm started immediately. They rode the government right from the beginning. I did 30 interviews with the press in less than a week. The supporters of Little Warriors called out the government for failing to do the right thing. Our supporters sent letters and posted videos on YouTube demanding the government step up and fund the Ranch. The government responded with bureaucratic language to back-pedal.

Love Comes Pouring In

Getting blindsided by the government brought about a mini low-point for me. By then, I took low points much more in stride. Still, I had my moments of anxiety and stress.

It was this specific incident, though, that elevated my commitment to surrender. During the government-funding affair, it was the only thing in my thoughts. One night, as my mind turned the event over and over, I received a phone call. Looking at the caller ID, I noticed the last name, LaBonte. Naturally, I assumed it was my friend, Irene LaBonte. We got on the phone, and she began asking me how I was doing. I answered from the heart; "It's a difficult time right now. The government just screwed us out of the funding, and I'm having a tough time with it."

I spoke in a familiar way and used my friend's name. That's when she cut me off to say, "Oh no, this is Eileen LaBonte," she said.

Eileen is the mother-in-law of my friend Irene LaBonte. I had never met her but soon found out that she was a supporter of Little Warriors.

"I saw on TV what the government is doing to you. It's not right, and I decided I wasn't going to let them get away with it. My husband is sick. He's dying of dementia, and I want to do a legacy project in his name. I can donate one million dollars to the Ranch," she said. She literally took my breath away. I gasped. And I knew right then and there that we were going to make it.

Eileen became like a mother to me over the next several months. Eileen is an incredible soul. Not only would she give the money so we could build the Ranch in her husband's name, but she was a force of nature once we started renovating and moving into the Ranch. That is why it is called the Little Warriors Be Brave Ranch by Ray LaBonte and Family.

We kept moving forward with our fundraising efforts. Dollars flowed in from new sources that heard about our mission. Progress was slow, but it was moving in the right direction. We put on a Be Brave Luncheon in Edmonton a couple of months later, continuing with our typical fundraising efforts. Only now we had the promise of the LaBonte donation with us, and this seemed to inspire others.

At the luncheon, a Calgary family approached me and asked how much more we needed to get the Ranch built.

"About a million more would do it," I said.

I turned back to my conversation and thought nothing of it until after the luncheon. Guests were getting up to leave when I noticed Laurie standing with the couple from Calgary. She was crying. "Laurie, what's the matter?" Through her tears Laurie replied, "I'll let them tell you." It was in that moment the couple told me, "We are donating the one million. We wired the money. You've got it. Build your Ranch."

The feeling that all this was happening without my input—to me rather than by me—flooded into my soul. God works, and all I had to do was trust. Here we were no more than a couple of weeks earlier being denied government funding, thinking that our project was done. Suddenly we had two million in funds.

It was time to buy the Ranch. A whole new reality opened up. I had pushed for years. Finally, it happened. Now we had momentum. We raised the additional funding quickly and finally the day came when we could purchase the property that would become the beautiful, one-of-a-kind, dream-come-true, Be Brave Ranch.

A friend reminded me that while this whole affair was happening I continued to say, "It's inevitable. It's going to happen. It's just a matter of time." It's true. I said these things to any and everyone that would listen, but looking back I'm not sure I completely believed them. I had doubts—plenty of them. I suppose my belief was greater than my doubts.

The Fun Part—Buying the Property

We had envisioned the Ranch for so long. Now we had a chance to sink our teeth into it. I was personally thrilled to play a role. I love properties, decorating spaces, and all things visual. I always had a vision for the Ranch. I didn't want a drab institutional feel.

I wanted the look and feel of a ranch—an oasis—where kids who had been through hell would feel safe. We wanted them to have a place where they could feel special, where they could heal and form bonds with their peers. A place to know they weren't alone as victims in spite of the trauma they'd experienced.

We wanted the kids to have the royal treatment in a sense, and so we set out to deliver it. We had to start with the right property. We found one around Caroline, Alberta, a small country town south of Edmonton, but in the end, it just wasn't right. It was a bit too far from Edmonton, and we felt we could do better.

A few people had told us to have a look at a site outside Sherwood Park, just to the east of Edmonton. Remember how I just finished saying we didn't want a drab institutional feel? This was it. The property would require work—a lot of work.

Did I mention that the facility had been vacant for four years? Infested with mice and whatever other animals moved in. It was 60,000 square feet on 120 acres, and there was just something about it. The location, the grounds and the building size—it had several things going for it. So, we bought it, knowing full well that the task of renovations ahead would be a major one.

The board of Little Warriors held a meeting to re-visit our provincial funding request and the so-called documentation issue. The $750,000 would go a long way to help with renovations. When the Minister asked for a face-to-face meeting we agreed. For the first time, we discussed the documentation at the meeting.

At the meeting, the Minister told me, "I don't care that you're a good marketer. I don't care about the letter campaigns or videos. You'll get your Ranch if we decide it's a good project."

I responded by telling him about the three promises I had made: To myself, to survivors and to God. I told him, "You didn't make my list."

It's hard to explain how satisfying it was to know that we'd already purchased the Ranch. I quietly leaned in, slid the deed for the property across the table to him and said, "You don't get to decide anything. Albertans have decided, and we already bought it cash."

We never have received any funding from the government.

The only way to make real change is to create a movement so strong it can't be ignored. People make a change. It's only people who have ever made a change.

Keep in mind that the Ranch is a clinically run and trauma informed facility. We have some of the most highly qualified trauma experts in the world, and we've put the trauma-informed program together with the experts at the University of Alberta, one of the most prestigious institutions in Canada. We're not some fly-by-the-seat-of-your-pants organization doing wacky, unproven therapies. The most advanced researchers and therapists in the field have developed our program. The government giving us money should be a complete no-brainer.

As much as the government's actions were despicable, it provided one memorable moment. The leader of the opposition and her fellow opposition party MLAs donated their salary raises to the Ranch. It offered a nice symbolic gesture showing the shortsightedness of the ruling government.

We appreciated the extra money, and it was nice to see that some people in the government cared.

Our Angel

Gary and I never thought we would adopt again but right in the middle of the government non-funding affair I received a call from a g[squared] staff member. There was a four-year-old little angel named Melissa, and she needed a home urgently. Her experiences had left her without the capacity or will to speak. That was a Friday evening. Gary and I had a few conversations over the weekend about what it would look like to add to our family of five.

On Monday we got a call that we were allowed to see her. She liked Gary immediately and the feeling was mutual. On Tuesday we went to visit her at her school. As we waited outside her classroom, I was on the phone with various media outlets discussing government funding issues.

It was adorable because she ran up to us. She was so happy to have people coming to see her.

We instantly fell in love with our new angel, and as always in situations like this, it completely put the other struggles into focus. We'd build our Ranch or we wouldn't. It was up to God. Yes, the community, the Little Warriors supporters and I could push and push. We had the will to do it, but ultimately, God would decide.

In the meantime, I realized there was plenty I could do at home. Melissa needed love, and Gary and I could do something about that. God gave her to us as a gift, and we received that gift with open arms. It pushed me to surrender a bit more, and as it turned out, that was just what I needed to do.

The Renovation and Massive Support

When we purchased the Ranch, I could officially declare that our movement was so strong that it couldn't be ignored. We made it happen with the efforts of thousands of people, and after a four-month process, it was a pleasure to own the property.

In December 2013, we triumphantly went out to the site, unlocked the doors, walked in and were promptly slapped in the face with the reality of what we just bought.

Have you ever made a purchase only to get the thing home and realize you'd just purchased a lot of work? The site had potential, which was why we bought it. It's 60,000 square feet and situated on a gorgeous property, but it was in horrible condition. Reality struck when we walked in that day.

Gary and several of our biggest supporters joined us when we walked the property for the first time. At one point, Eileen La-Bonte looked over at me and said, "Glori, are you okay?" I felt utterly overwhelmed by the work ahead of us. I had never done a renovation before. I mean I'd hired the odd painter. I put wallpaper up once, but it was crooked. Taking in the enormity of the task in front of us, I had a mini anxiety attack. Eileen could see it in my face.

I told her my fears, and like the second mother she is to me, she gave me a little hug and told me we'd get through this. As it turned out, I'd need all of her support and much more to pull it off.

The funds Little Warriors had weren't remotely enough money to get the entire facility professionally restored. We always knew it would require a community effort. However, we underestimated just how much of a community effort it would be. Again, I'd have to surrender. I had to trust that this thing would get done because the reality of the situation was that it would require a massive effort and plenty of further monetary assistance.

I wouldn't say it was conscious at the time, but I adopted an attitude of trusting all problems would be solved. Every time we needed something I'd ask God, put the word out there and then the result would come in. Throughout the entire process, we always got what we needed—starting with the volunteers. As soon as we took possession, we put a call out for help. We would need a lot of volunteers and we weren't disappointed. People came in droves—every single weekend that we needed them, they would come. That very first weekend it was forty below zero, and the volunteers showed up by the dozen. They carried out garbage, hauled away old rotten mattresses, tore down crumbling walls, and did everything we asked them to do.

We gutted that place. Only the bones of the original site remained. We replaced the electrical, the plumbing, the roofing, the fire suppression system and every other thing except for the foundation and the structure. We installed a security system, and named the outdoor rink after our fellow survivor and hero, Theo Fleury. There is an art room, therapy rooms of all types, rooms for the kids who come along with a guardian. You name it—we pretty much built or installed it all from scratch. And it was mostly done by volunteers and donations.

In many cases where the work was technical and complicated, we received deeply discounted rates. Take, for instance, the fire safety system. The building's previous operator had their fire safety system grandfathered. We tore out all the old stuff, so we were forced to update to the most modern type of fire system as demanded by the building safety codes. The fire inspector delivered the news, and we were more than a little bit surprised to find out that it would cost $100,000. I had no idea where we'd get the money, yet a day later we received another donation from Eileen LaBonte for that amount. She was on site that day and heard what happened. She wrote a cheque to get the whole thing done.

We needed a new roof. That's a massive, expensive job on a 60,000 square foot building. Acron Roofing and Jayson Global stepped up and did the job for us. Durabuilt Windows and Doors replaced all the windows and doors in all four of our buildings. All of the furnaces needed cleaning, so Alberta Carpet and Furnace Cleaning came through and did them all for free. We required vehicles for the kids at the Ranch, so I emailed the owners of Go Auto and

Driving Force. Within a week, they both stepped up and had vans ready for us to pick up.

Every step of the way, we received more and more donations wherever we needed them, both in the form of cash and donated work and expertise. Parkwood Master Builder, a local Edmonton-based home building company, offered a ton of its staff to oversee and execute a large portion of the build.

I'm leaving out so many incredible people and businesses. There isn't enough space to tell each of their stories, but you can find them all listed on the Little Warriors website.

A mere list doesn't do them justice. Each of these beautiful donors was so incredibly timely, too. They answered the call. Whenever a need arose, some new hero would arrive. I think this was the greatest lesson in surrendering I got through the entire process. The world is a remarkable place.

Speaking of heroes, I need to talk about the volunteers. They kept coming, weekend after weekend, for nine months straight. I got to know some incredible people, people who care a whole bunch, people whose efforts protected me from cynicism.

The people—thank God for the people. People are real and they care.

There is not enough space here to thank each of our volunteers and donors individually. There have been thousands upon thousands over the years.

I do want to mention a couple of volunteers specifically, though. Jason Paquette showed up on the first volunteer day of building the Ranch, and I don't think he missed a day for the several months it took to renovate the place. Jason brought friends and just did whatever we needed him to do. Sandblasting was one task not many people wanted to do. Jason stepped up. He has helped us so much, and I'm forever grateful for his whatever-it-takes attitude. Little Warriors volunteers like Jason do it for the kids. They drive themselves by love for the kids that need our support rather than their fears and doubts.

Dawn Taylor volunteered every weekend and poured her heart and soul into the renovations.

Cory White oversaw the renovation of the Ranch. She literally lived and slept there for 10 months. Everything that could be wrong in a building was wrong. All of the rooms required sanding and Cory rallied her family to sand every room. A hundred volunteers would show up everyday and she would put them all to work. Cory made sure we opened on time.

Chris Erickson was the first male to be a spokesperson in our ad campaigns. It's not easy for men to speak up as a survivor of abuse but he courageously shared his story.

Another volunteer couple is Brian and Brenda Smith. These two were there throughout the entire renovation. They were quiet, hard workers who never wavered in their support. In particular, they took a special interest in what we called our "magic room." It's a unique room at the Ranch designed to let the kids dream. One of the worst consequences of abuse is often that an abused kid starts to think they're not special or that they don't deserve good things in life.

The magic room is a place designed to let them see the possibilities and magic in life, and the kids love it. There is a little tiny door that leads into the room. Inside it's stuffed with toys. Each kid gets to go into the magic room and pick a toy they want to take. I love it, and I'm so thankful to Brian, Brenda and all the volunteers.

Support and Love

I'm most proud of the love. Little Warriors is founded on love. We didn't know whether or not we'd ever be able to raise the millions of dollars and get the Ranch built. From myself down to the little kids selling cookies, it took the love and effort of thousands of people to get the Ranch built.

In some cases, it was me who needed love and support. Eileen LaBonte started as a donor but became a second mother to me. Watching this 70-year-old woman work during the renovations, by lugging mattresses through the snow and cold, kept me going everyday. And Gary has been there for every moment. I can't say enough about Ilan, too. She's a fantastic friend that provides a shoulder to cry on when necessary but will call you out when you need it.

And then there's Heather, a woman who's become a close friend over the past couple of years. Heather stepped up several times as both a donor and volunteer when most needed. But more importantly, Heather has been a friend. We laugh and have fun together, and we talk about everything. When the going got tough on countless occasions through the fundraising and building of the Ranch, there was nothing more valuable than being able to relax and enjoy life for a few hours.

I'm so thankful for all those that supported the Ranch and me personally. Life is entirely about relationships. Without the thousands of supportive people in my life, none of this would have been possible.

We Did It!

The grand opening was celebrated with over 800 people and provided fun for all who had contributed money and effort. It was also a great chance to share this incredible health victory with the media and public. The day was unseasonably cold but the weather couldn't put a chill on how exciting it was.

I soaked up hundreds of hugs and smiles all day long. We did it! The dream that all those early naysayers believed would never come true was in full sight right before my eyes. I'd suffered a few battle scars from fights I never wanted with the government, but they were worth it. Even the fact that no government officials showed up at the opening of the treatment centre for Alberta kids couldn't bring me down.

All I ever wanted was to build a place where kids could come and be healed. Going to war, protected only by my vulnerability and authenticity, was a small price to pay for the opportunity to change lives.

The effort got us to the grand opening, which was reminiscent of the whole renovation process. There we were, on September 27, 2014, celebrating the opening day of the Ranch, and facing the same problem we had for the whole renovation.

We didn't have enough money to run the facility. Building it was one task, but unless we could pay the clinical, food service and maintenance staff, this beautiful dream would never be able to help the kids.

Our plan, as always, was to dive in and raise the money. My intention was to pray and trust. I was genuinely concerned, but by then knew that I just had to do two things. First, I had to give my best effort. Second, I had to surrender.

The night before the grand opening, I was having dinner with friends from Vancouver. I let slip that we needed to ramp up the funding to ensure the Ranch would be operational for the coming year.

The next day at the grand opening, my friends pulled me aside for a chat.

"Don't worry about the first year," they said.

"What do you mean," I said.

"God told my wife and I to give you a million dollars. You said you'd need about a million more to ensure the first year is taken care of right? We'll take care of it," he said.

I couldn't believe my ears. For the fourth time in two years, I was surprised by a massive donation from a loving supporter. This movement had officially inspired millions—people and dollars. Now we could run the Ranch for the entire first year without worry, helping and healing more than 100 kids.

On the heels of that conversation, Irene LaBonte let me know she would donate $100,000 for one of the homes to house the children. She named it Mertz House. Likewise, Ryan Shoemaker stepped up and donated $100,000 to name the second home, Shoemaker House.

We would have to continually raise funds in the coming years to ensure we could help kids into the future, but with these donations, I could officially say we did it. The big day we fought for had come. The Ranch was now a significant force.

Kids finally had a place to get better with the care and support of the thousands of people from around the world.

The Real Big Day

The grand opening made me happy, but one of the most satisfying moments of my life came when the first of the kids arrived with their friends and family.

I wasn't going to miss that day for the world.

I think I cried non-stop for the entire day. My tears of joy came at the thought and sight of this first cohort of kids finally getting the help and support they deserve. The people who care spoke up with their voices, their money and their effort. Through this combined push, we built this remarkable facility and filled it with the top experts and staff available—all for the kids.

Sexually abused children often internalize self-blame and self-hatred from a young age. They often don't believe they are worthy of good things happening to them. Through support, rehabilitation and the care of others, they can turn that around. They can develop self-love and genuine belief in their value.

Be Brave Ranch represented a step in that direction. The message to kids, who've experienced a world of hurt and pain is, "Somebody cares about you." Not just somebody—a lot of people care.

A couple of moments during the kids' first day sum up my joy: I remember seeing one of the boys, after walking around and getting himself accustomed to the place, turned to his mom and said, "There's a chef!" It symbolized the spirit of, "They care." He was blown away by the detail that we had put into the Ranch.

His words brought tears to my eyes.

Another moment unfolded in the art room. A little boy from the first cohort of kids was there when I walked in. He asked me, "Who are you?"

"I'm the founder."

"What's a founder?"

"I'm the lady who started this place."

Quite innocently, he stated, "Why would you do that?"

"Well I'm a survivor too and I wanted to build a place for kids who have experienced child sexual abuse like you. I wanted to give them a beautiful place to go and heal."

He replied, "How much money did you have to raise?"

"A lot of money."

"Well why would you build a ranch for us? Why wouldn't you just keep the money and buy a big house for yourself?"

"Because you are more important. Because you and other kids like you deserve to get better."

These survivor kids deserve so much. I know the Ranch will make a massive difference in the lives of those lucky enough to attend our programs.

It was all I ever wanted. No recognition. No battles with the government. The only thing I wanted was to have that place for those deserving kids to go and get better. Thousands of other people wanted the same outcome. And when I articulated this vision through Little Warriors, they got behind it.

We did it.

I slept like a victorious warrior that night.

CHAPTER 19

BE BRAVE RANCH—A SAFE PLACE WHERE COURAGE CONQUERS FEAR

"I just wish people would realize that anything's possible if you try; dreams are made possible if you try."

— Terry Fox

First In The World

I see everything through two filters:

1. What is feasible?

2. How can we make it happen?

Trauma-focused, cognitive behaviour therapy is the foundation piece of the Ranch program. In 2013, Dr. Peter Silverstone and his team began developing an integrated plan for treating child sexual abuse. He took what had proven to be successful and brought the pieces together into a holistic program.

In 2014 the Board of Little Warriors commissioned the University of Alberta's Faculty of Medicine and Dentistry to develop an intensive, dedicated and multi-modal treatment for child sexual abuse survivors (aged 8-12). Dr. Silverstone led the charge and rallied a clinical team to assist in the development.

Our team designed a novel, intensive and comprehensive one-year program for children aged 8-12. The program involves four periods during which the children stay at the Be Brave Ranch (with parents or guardian whenever possible) for an initial period of three weeks followed by three further one-week periods (at 4, 8, and 12 months). It was quickly determined that the length of each round would need to be expanded to four weeks for the initial stay followed by two weeks for the second, third and fourth rounds of therapy. During these periods they receive more than 200 hours of therapy and in-between the children and their families are supported by weekly outpatient group sessions alongside peers who have experienced similar trauma.

The goals were to improve symptoms of Post-traumatic Stress Disorder, Depression, Anxiety, Quality of Life, Self-esteem and Attachment. Our clinical framework is built upon ensuring a therapeutic milieus (within the Cabin environments) and using evidence based clinical practices and therapies including TF-CBT, group therapy, individual trauma treatment, family therapy, play therapy, expressive therapies and animal assisted therapy.

In reflecting on the evolution of Be Brave Ranch, Dr. Silverstone says, "Glori's drive got this done. She was open to novel suggestions. We developed a truly unique and very interesting program that is tailor-made to the children."

My admiration of Dr. Silverstone may sound over the top but I love him so much. God brought him into my life at just the right time. Our approach faced relentless opposition but we warriored on.

The process certainly wasn't linear. Our program progressed through several iterations. We faced realities once the program was functional and made changes as required. Over time, personnel changed and new personnel brought in fresh perspectives.

Dr. Silverstone chairs our Scientific and Clinical Oversight Committee along with Dr. Andrew Greenshaw, Dr. Vincent Agyapong, Dr. Yifeng Wei, MA, PhD, Dr. Hannah Pazderka, PhD, and Matthew Reeson, B.Sc.

Our Clinical team is currently headed up by Dr. Wanda Polzin, MA, RSW, EdD, Clinical Director and her team of Melanie Jonkman, M.Ed and Allison Boudreau, M.Ed Trauma Therapists (both Registered Psychologists); Cheryl Horn, Art Therapist; Deborah Johansson, Registered Psychologist; Eileen Bona, M.Ed., Equine Therapist, Owner and Founder of Dreamcatcher Association and Rugby our therapy dog.

Dr. Polzin, MA, RCSW, EdD, is responsible for the program's clinical outcomes. Outcomes may sound mundane. Not in the least. They are the lifeblood of hope, fulfillment and funding. Before employment with the Ranch, Dr. Polzin worked at CASA, Child, Adolescent and Family Mental Health in Edmonton. The innovative and trauma-informed approach of the Ranch caught her attention and led to her shared devotion in the cause. Clinicians under Dr. Polzin's guidance, make use of 12 intervention modalities.

Integral to the modalities is the use of Animal Assisted Therapy. That's where Rugby, a yellow lab, comes in. Everyone loves Rugby. Dr. Polzin is Rugby's handler. Rugby graduated from two years of extensive training at Dogs With Wings as a therapy dog. Dr. Polzin was trained to work with Rugby. Rugby and Dr. Polzin are co-therapists. The children at Be Brave Ranch were their first assignment.

Rugby interacts with the children in therapy sessions. He is trained to pick up on behavioural and emotional cues. Rugby will lie down beside a child whom he feels needs support or lay his head on their lap so they can stroke him while sharing in a session. Rugby is present when the children have discussions about boundaries and talk about their abuse. Rugby has even attended court and sat on the stand with children. He has a therapeutic knack of "grounding" children by gently laying across their feet when that have to stand up and talk about their trauma. Some children suffered abuse in the presence of an animal or animals were used as a part of their abuse. Rugby helps kids see friendly animals in a new light and develop trust and affection for them.

Healthy Outcomes for Adolescents

The Be Brave Ranch (BBR) supports and treats children and adolescents (who have a history of sexual abuse trauma) to move forward in their lives (and in their families and within their communities) in more positive, functional ways through support from a bio-psycho-social-spiritual perspective. These outcomes are achieved by building upon resiliencies through strengthening existing abilities and motivation and developing new understandings and skills in the areas of distress tolerance, emotional regulation, mindfulness, psychological and emotional safety, healthy interpersonal relationships, problem-solving, conflict management, communication, self-awareness and reflection and caregiver supports and functioning.

Dr. Polzin introduced a program for girls aged 13-16 in October 2018. Five adolescents made up the first cohort. They use the same treatment rooms at the Ranch and live in a cabin all their own. In addition to the modalities, these young women learn life skills, employment skills and how to write a resume.

Each youth has an Individualized Care Plan that is co-created along with them, their identified support system(s), as well as the Be Brave Interdisciplinary Team. Together, the youth and their Care Team discover abilities to achieve self-established goals. This discovery process promotes the growth that marks their movement through an intense intermittent care model as well as readiness for "completion" of the program. The team initially works with the child and his/her family in Phase 1 to establish safety, ensure knowledge through ongoing psycho-education, conduct thorough bio-psycho-social assessments, and begin working to calm the activation/arousal states. Phase 2 involves trauma processing, ongoing arousal de-activation and reinforcements of safety factors, while Phase 3 builds on enhancing safety and ongoing therapeutic gains and resiliency supports.

Together, as a multidisciplinary team, they create a trauma-informed therapeutic milieu characterized by sensitivity to individual needs. In this environment the adolescent and their family/caregiver can develop and experience competence and success. The highly trained BBR Clinical Care Team supports children and adolescents through implementing leading practices to scaffold strategies relating to their individual areas of concern through various evidence-based interventions. Individual therapy sessions, group therapy, as well as Family/Caregiver Therapy and Supports are built into the program.

From the research and the outcome measures of the Clinical Programming, it's been found that upon completion of the BBR program, adolescents and their families:

- demonstrate greater understanding of their present situation and past negative coping strategies.

- demonstrate healthy, adaptive methods of functioning individually, within the family and within the wider social context.

- report improved sense of self, self-worth and self-esteem.

- demonstrate improvements in interpersonal/family relationships.

- report successful community linkages into appropriate community resources and/or alternative school or vocational placement.

- improve in bio-psycho-social functioning (improve mental health, physical health awareness and functioning).

- recognize their strengths and resiliencies to move forth in a happier, healthier manner.

The Outcome Measures that are captured are done so with the support of the (external) Scientific and Clinical Council members. There is ongoing work to evaluate the treatment program through outcome (pre/post) measures of both the youth as well as the caregiver. The following information is collected through ongoing standardized protocols related to (but not limited to) client and caregiver demographic information, client and caregiver satisfaction, the nature of the trauma experienced, history of Adverse Childhood Experiences and Events (ACES), PTSD, Quality of Life, Substance Use and Mis-use/Risk, Depression, Anxiety, Self-Esteem, Resiliency.

As a leading practice, the Little Warriors/Be Brave Ranch clinical framework is evidence-informed and focuses on key areas:

1. Application of Current Brain Science and Neurodevelopment; a strengths-based, resiliency approach. We believe in building research into practice.

2. Reducing Toxic Stress for the adolescents through building upon strengths individually, within the caregiver setting, as well as within the larger community.

3. Trauma-Informed interventions for the adolescent, their caregivers/families and staff within the program.

4. Evidence based programming to serve individual needs as well as the needs within the family system.

Wrapping Them With Love

Children come to the Be Brave Ranch for more than 200 hours of therapy over one year. When children arrive, they become part of a cohort. Each cohort consists of a maximum of six children. They learn together, play together, and go through therapy together for a month. Throughout the year, children return to the Ranch for three additional 12-day stays to continue their face-to-face therapy and reconnect in person with their cohort. There is intense bonding. The 8-12-year-old girls love painting each other's nails. Kids who felt all alone discover peers who can relate on an empathetic level.

On the first day of the program, the girls and boys can choose a brightly coloured quilt. The quilts are warm, soft, and comforting. They're made with a massive dose of "TLC—tender loving care" and donated to the Ranch. Many quilt-makers write a heartfelt letter to go along with the quilt. The messages are filled with hope and are a favourite of the kids. A child chooses his or her very own quilt and one of the letters. When a child goes home, they take the quilt with them to link their time at the Ranch with their home life.

The words on one of the quilts sum up the hopes for each child,

"Let me keep you safe and warm,
I'll snuggle you from dusk to dawn,
May heaven's light shine from above,
And wrap you up in strength and love."

Staff members conduct constant assessment and research of the programming. The Ranch is trauma-informed, culturally sensitive, understands and recognizes gender differences and supports the individual as well as being family-centred.

Thirty to 35 percent of the children at Be Brave Ranch are Indigenous. Excellence with Indigenous services involves the inclusion of lived experience and having families and communities participate in the development and ongoing evaluation of the program.

Be Brave Ranch is fun but its not easy for the children.

One girl wasn't sure she could stay in the program. Every day she was texting her family. I told her, "I'm a survivor. I'm the same as you." I shared about my grandfather's abuse. I told her why we built the Ranch. "The Ranch is a gift to change the trajectory of your life so that you don't end up like me with lots of anxiety and

PTSD. It doesn't mean that I can't do great things, but it doesn't mean that I don't have mental health issues."

I took her little face in both hands and said, "Honey, you've got this. Look me in the eyes right now sweetheart and tell me you've got this. Because I'm telling you, you don't know what lies ahead. Be Brave Ranch is your chance to live a whole-hearted life. I am an older version of you who never got help."

Kids love being at the Ranch. Weekends are spent entirely playing, and weekdays are comprised of therapy with some play. The program was designed to be an experience that the children would take with them and remember for life.

Program results speak for themselves in the lives of children, like Seaver.

Seaver's Story

Seaver was eight years old. He clearly understood that if ever he said anything to anyone about the abuse, his mom and his sister would die. And then he would be next. Seaver stayed silent. In his mind staying silent was the most courageous thing a boy could do. For over six months, he endured sexual abuse. He was like 75 percent of sexual abuse survivors in Canada, victimized by a member of his or her family. However, in Seaver's case, two family members took advantage of his innocence.

Seaver's five-year-old sister suffered sexual abuse from the same family members. Day after day, the two lived in fear that if one of them accidentally let their abuse slip out, their sibling and mother would be murdered in front of them. That would be the last image they would ever see. Their paternal grandmother and father made sure that they could continue abusing Seaver and his sister with impunity. Yes, their grandmother and father.

Like many Canadian boys, Seaver dreamed about playing in the NHL. He is gifted with excellent hockey sense and above-average skills for his age. At school, he was aiming for A's, enjoyed pizza and burgers and liked making people laugh. The abuse stole his confidence and ate away at his insides. He was bullied at school and grew more anxious with each passing day. His only goal—to stay alive and help his sister survive.

In the early summer of 2012, Seaver told his mom he would like to visit his aunt who lived on the Eastern seaboard in the U.S. His mom had no idea that he was trying to get away from his abusers. He was willing to face a cross-continent flight, alone, as an eight-year-old. Seaver's only anxiety was leaving his sister behind. He made his mom promise not to let his sister go to Grandma's or Dad's house by herself. One month into his absence, Seaver's sister let their secret slip.

When he returned home his mom asked if he had been abused. He lied to her and then stayed silent. A month later, he suffered an emotional breakdown and confessed the abuse to his mom. The siblings' confessions would result in a long, expensive court battle for custody. The police chose to take the word of the abusers over the children. The Crown believed the evidence was sufficient to prosecute but did not want to put the kids through the experience of cross-examination. As with 98% of abuse cases in Canada, the abusers went free, and legal fees saddled the innocent with debt.

Over the following three years, Seaver's mom sought help for her children from the Elizabeth Fry Society, psychologists and a psychiatrist. Her Internet searches for additional help led her to an online documentary called "Building Brave." A brand new support centre for child sexual abuse survivors was under construction outside Edmonton. There was hope! The next day she was on the phone pleading to have her son become one of the first children to participate. When the Be Brave Ranch opened its doors to the first cohort in 2014, Seaver was there.

Today, Seaver is a 6'2" young man. He captains his hockey team and is their leading scorer. He developed an interest in baseball. The heat he could put on a baseball garnered attention from scouts and earned him a roster spot on a college-prep team playing in the U.S. He's a big fan of Drake, raps his lines, and makes people laugh with his sense of humour.

Seaver's mom says, "My kids were murdered. Everything was taken away from them. Be Brave Ranch gave them their lives back."

Touring the Ranch

Let me take you on a tour of the Be Brave Ranch and introduce you to some of our world-class practitioners. We have around-the-clock security at the entrance gate, ensuring the safety of the children on site. On the inside there are picnic tables for nice summer days. There is a fenced-in basketball court and hockey rink. The Edmonton Oilers and their former opponent, Theo Fleury of the Calgary Flames, are partners in supporting the Ranch. I was happy to name the rink in my fellow warrior's honour, "The Theo Fleury Rink of Courage."

We wanted the first steps into the reception area to convince any anxious little one that this is a child-friendly building. A message drawn on a chalkboard in bright colours says, "Welcome." The brick features, wood flooring and brightly lit entrance speak volumes to parents about the care and excellence that went into the design.

Be Brave Ranch employees like front desk administrators Karen and Miranda or transitional coordinator workers like Megan and Jill are in place to make good first impressions. After a brief amount of paperwork, a child and their parent(s) take a tour of the facility. Tour guides save the best for last—the Be Brave Ranch cabins.

We wanted the Be Brave Ranch experience to be unforgettable for all the right reasons. Entering one of the log cabins, kids take in the pinewood walls, airy windows, sloped ceiling, bold support beam and dark wood flooring. Black leather couches adorned with bright throw cushions promise relaxing times.

Family-style breakfasts are one of the ways to help children connect with each other and their caregivers. A long, rectangular table with a wooden top becomes Breakfast Central every day. Best of all, each child has their very own bedroom. And they can bring pictures and personal items to make their space feel like home. Staff members provide 24-hour support and assure children they are not on their own.

Design features that hallmark Be Brave Ranch include dedicated space for each of the 12 intervention therapies offered to the children. Because children respond to different forms of treatment, using a multi-modal approach helps discover which treatment works best for each child.

There is a Yoga Room, kept in pristine condition, and used only for daily Yoga to ensure the energy in the space is calming and soothing. The drawings hanging on the walls of the Art Therapy Room tell the story of feelings and thoughts, created artistically by the children.

The Music Room inspires children to get out their creative energy and work together to make new sounds. Drumming, in particular, assists children in regulating their emotional state as the beat soothes the nervous system. Every instrument has a story. In fact, the entire Music Room is a story. I shared the story earlier of a 19-year old woman who died by suicide. When we built the Ranch we dedicated the Music Room in her memory. Her mom and stepfather became incredible supporters of the Ranch. When her stepfather passed away all of the memorial donations were made to the Ranch.

Typical of the donations is an upright piano that sits along one wall. Don Vaugeois owned a piano shop. He learned about an autistic girl, a little warrior named Halie, who loves music. She writes songs, and when she hears a piece on the piano, she never forgets it. Don donated the Be Brave Ranch piano and dedicated it to Halie.

As mentioned earlier, when a child arrives at the Ranch, he or she is allowed to come to the Magic Room and pick out one new, boxed toy. The toy helps a child feel like they have something that's theirs in this new place.

A Play Room is brightly coloured, with games galore, providing children their right to play. The words written in script on one wall reminds them of the power of a smile. "Because of your smile, you make life more beautiful."

An Aboriginal Room is used for drumming or engaging in cultural practices.

The Family Lounge is the most versatile space in the facility. It's used for everything from parent visits to tea parties.

At least once a week, children are treated to a movie night with popcorn. Cozy blankets covering leather couches provide a comfortable setting. Children get to vote on their choice of a movie to relax and process all of the hard work they do.

Children spend two hours every day in the Therapy Room, participating with their cohort. Plush toys fill the storage shelves, and welcome kids to sit with them on the couches and chairs. All the play and therapy is bound to make a kid hungry. Children and families enjoy delicious, kid-friendly lunches and dinners in the dining room.

I'm so proud of our professional clinical team working with the children. They come from various backgrounds, including psychology, social work, early childhood development, expressive art therapy, and recreation therapy. Several members of the team have doctoral and masters level qualifications.

The health and well being of the Ranch staff are paramount to the work. A Staff Sanctuary is maintained to provide a calming atmosphere in which the team can debrief and obtain support.

Final Closure

In January 2014, I received news that Wib passed away from lung cancer.

When my mom told me I just broke down in tears. I was confused. I associate crying with sadness, but there is no way I could be sad at this man's death, could I? I asked myself, "Why am I crying? This rotten dude drops dead of lung cancer, and here I am crying? It didn't make sense."

But, it does make sense. When you're a survivor, you hold onto so much emotion. Even after having worked so long on releasing these emotions and moving on, there was still so much bottled up inside me. I wasn't so much crying because I was upset at his death. I was angry at his life, everything he represented and the course it set my life on.

How can a single person have such a massive effect on one's life?

Here's the best part about the rollercoaster ride of his death. Not only was I upset, I also got mad at myself for getting angry. Oh, the joys of overcoming abuse!

Thankfully, I had coping strategies by then. So, I sat with this upset and pain for a bit, and said to myself, "What he did was wrong, but I took what he did and turned it into something good." Since the first moment of abuse, this man played such a massive role in my life—for better or for worse—and I felt his presence every day since that first day. From sheer terror to hatred, haunting my dreams, Wib was there, lurking in the back of my psyche.

As an independent adult, I knew that he couldn't harm me, but subconsciously he was still a threat to my safety. However, after processing, I finally felt his evil presence disappear. A huge weight lifted off my shoulders. It was total and final closure.

A couple of days later, I was in Warrior mode again. I searched for Wib's obituary in the Miramichi Newspaper and was appalled. The obituary painted a picture of him as some saintly man. It's not surprising, I suppose. It's not like my grandmother would want to portray the truth to the world about the kind of man he indeed was.

What was even more appalling to me were the comments from others, gushing about what a "nice man" Wib was. Surely they knew of his record of sexual abuse. All I could do was what I'd been doing for years now—use my two-pronged approach of fighting back on the one hand and letting go on the other.

In the spirit of fighting back, I wrote my obituary for Wib. In my version, the title of the obituary was, "Sex Offender Dies." This man had gotten away with his crimes enough in life. I didn't want him to get off scot-free in death, too.

Everything I had done up until his death was fuelled by fighting back against his abuse. From the moment of his death onward, all I have accomplished was fuelled by my desire for good.

I found the timing of his death to be most interesting. He dropped dead 90 days after we opened the Ranch. It was as though his evil spirit and the spirit of good were locked in a battle.

When the Ranch opened, good won and evil lost.

CHAPTER 20

A NEW HOPE

"The secret of change is to focus all your energy, not on fighting the old, but on building the new."

— *Socrates*

Building The New

Be Brave Ranch became a spiritual oasis where a survivor would be given the tools they need to heal their body, heart, spirit and mind.

We believed and worked and waited to see the expected outcomes. The lives of survivors and the life of the Ranch depended on them.

Data is like gold. Clinical data results were collected, hoping to confirm the success of the Be Brave Ranch treatment program.

On April 18, 2016 Dr. Silverstone released the report from the Journal of Child and Adolescent Behaviour to the press. The headlines declared, "Be Brave Ranch clinical results show improved outcomes for child sexual abuse survivors." The byline enthused, "researchers say stunning results from the Little Warriors Be Brave Ranch in helping child sexual abuse survivors heal could revolutionize sexual assault therapy."

This was the realization of our dream. Eight years of effort spent trying to bring the Ranch to fruition was yielding astounding results for vulnerable children.

After the initial 28-day stay, children ages 8-12 show a 25 percent reduction in child PTSD scores and a significant reduction in symptoms of Depression and Anxiety. Once the children have completed the full yearlong program only 29 percent meet the criteria for PTSD, down from 73 percent who had full-spectrum PTSD.

The four-week intervention program was found to significantly reduce the psychological impacts of child sexual abuse. As the first intensive program to demonstrate such clinical impact, these results suggested the potential for a breakthrough for the lasting mental health of child sexual abuse survivors and for the far-reaching outcomes of this severe trauma.

The results included highly significant reductions in:

Post-Traumatic Stress Disorder (PTSD),
Depression,
Anxiety,
Suicide,
Alcoholism, and
Addiction—things that happen to kids who don't have programs.

Dr. Silverstone explained that focusing on rates of experienced PTSD is critical in gauging the positive outcomes of treatment, as PTSD has been shown to have long-term implications that can significantly "alter the life trajectory of the child." The data also showed a significant reduction in reported Depression and Anxiety.

These initial results demonstrate that the application of multiple, intensive treatment methods can impact the individual and overarching outcomes of child sexual abuse. In layman's terms, we have uncovered new hope for this horrific crime. I really believe this is the start of a paradigm shift in treatment.

Hope Furthered

There has been new scientific literature that continues to be published in the field of Child Sexual Abuse by the treatment team and Scientific and Clinical Council, noting from the Canadian Journal of Child and Adolescent Psychiatry that suggests even more positive improvement in the short-term and long-term.

The Adolescent Program results show improvement in outcome measures and decrease in symptoms related to Anxiety, PTSD and Depression after the initial 2-week treatment round for twenty-seven adolescent girls.

The Child Program (ages 8-12) results show very gratifying improvements in self-report outcome measures for PTSD, Anxiety, Depression, Quality of Life and Self-esteem, and preliminary evidence suggests they may continue to increase during the 12 months spent in the program.

Kids are better at school and life. Additionally, Be Brave's intensive and comprehensive treatment program significantly improves cognitive abilities, and resiliency. This has been found in research conducted along with MyCognition and MyCQ. The program not only supports healing of PTSD, anxiety, and depression, but there are also clinically significant improvements in frontal lobe functioning (involved with things like problem solving, impulse control, and other higher cognitive functions).

The Be Brave Ranch program will lead to profound long-term benefits including:

- A greatly reduced risk of future drug and alcohol use.
- Increased performance in school.
- A decrease in school dropout rates.
- A decrease in suicide rates.
- A decrease in interactions with the criminal justice system.

Government Stewardship Needed

Successful programs cannot only reduce the suffering of child survivors, but can also significantly lower future health care costs by changing the health trajectory of children.

Preliminary calculations and research conducted by the Scientific and Clinical Committee indicate that for every dollar invested in the Little Warriors Be Brave Ranch, $10 is saved in social services and healthcare costs over five years. For every $1 million invested, $10 million is saved over five years. Normally, the return on investment equals savings of 1:5 or 1:10. We are looking at significantly larger savings, as our numbers are even higher.

Presently we operate without government support, relying on generous donors. None of the $30 million dollars designated annually in Alberta to supporting child sexual abuse survivors goes to Be Brave Ranch.

It makes good sense that an investment of provincial tax dollars in the Be Brave Ranch would save lives and save taxpayers' money.

Be Brave Ranch exists because the kids are lovable. We love them and we care. They deserve better because they did nothing wrong.

Our kids need the chance to get well. The Be Brave Ranch is the only world-class centre that can give them that chance.

CHAPTER 21
THROWING ROPES

"Courage: the most important of all the virtues because without courage, you can't practice any other virtue consistently."

— *Maya Angelou*

Seeing the Lesson in Rock Bottom

I look back now and on so many of my life events, and the meaning becomes clear. So many were tests I ultimately passed. God slapped me in the face with the lessons I needed.

Having the court case thrown out, considering suicide and the Hoffman Process were all essential building blocks for the next phase. They helped form the person I am today. They each helped with my healing.

I've been in the hole of depression, unhappiness and anxiety. I know how horrible it is. I'll be forever grateful for the people that threw me ropes when I was in that hole. I want to throw ropes to others who might still be struggling.

Do I still have bad days? Of course, and I'm confident that my healing journey isn't remotely close to complete. But I'm on the path now, and there's no way I'm coming off. I know what works, and I'm sticking to it.

Everyone's healing journey is different, but there are some consistencies shared by most people on the path. The rope we use to climb out of the hole is made up of several different strands.

Strand #1 – Hitting Rock Bottom

The first strand of the rope is hitting rock bottom, which for me was multifaceted. Near suicide, losing in court and struggling through a recession were all separate but connected rock bottoms. It was a whole period of rock bottom.

Each time I hit rock bottom was a new beginning of healing. I used each of these points to start climbing back to where I wanted to be. Hands down, the lowest point and absolute rock bottom for me was my near suicide. It pushed me to the most significant healing. There were so many times along the way I could have given up. I'm so grateful I didn't.

If you're in the hole, look for rock bottom. It looks different for everyone. Rock bottom is that moment when you stop everything, look at your life and realize this has to change now. For fellow abuse survivor and advocate in the fight against childhood sexual abuse Theo Fleury, it was a night where he held a gun in his mouth after his millionth bender. For me, it was a long period that culminated with suicidal thoughts.

Hitting rock bottom is the first step, but alone it's not enough. Many people hit rock bottom and never leave. Hitting rock bottom isn't magic. But with rock bottom often comes a commitment to real change. That's when the work begins.

Strand #2 – Courage

After hitting rock bottom comes courage. Once you're at your low point, it's easy to wallow there forever. These are the people who choose to stay in the hole, unable to muster the courage to change.

If you lack courage, don't worry. We can build courage over time, and make no mistake, it takes great courage to climb out of the hole. Wallowing is the easy way out. It requires no change, and it allows people to continue to blame others.

Having courage doesn't mean putting on a fierce face and saying others haven't hurt you. It means you're responsible for your own well-being. Most of all, it means being willing to do the work to grow.

For me, courage showed up several times. Courage was looking in the mirror and realizing it wasn't Gary's fault in our marriage. Courage was looking at my body, realizing I wasn't healthy and doing something about it.

Courage was admitting I was leading out of fear and that I was to blame for losing Freeda and the executive team. Most of all, courage realized my suicidal thoughts meant I had to change immediately. The courage came back halfway through the Hoffman Process. A moment of decision is a powerful moment. Often we decide to make a quick change, and these are the changes that quickly fizzle out. Think about how few people follow through with New Year's resolutions. It's the easily won changes that don't last. The ones you have to fight for with thousands of small acts are the changes that last a lifetime.

Choosing to get back on the path every day takes courage.

Strand #3 – Self-Work

Once you've got the courage, you're ready to move forward with healing. Many people go looking for a magic pill at this point, a simple solution, and a group to take their mind off the problem, a new hobby, or any other number of distractions. Don't get me wrong, I'm not saying there's anything wrong with these things, but there's no magic pill to true healing. There's only hard work. It's self-work though, and therefore is the most rewarding kind of work.

Without committing to this self-work, there's no forward progress. Imagine if I'd found the courage after nearly running my car off the road and then said, "I'm too busy to do the self-work." My healing would have stalled, and I'd have gone back to exactly where I was.

What does the self-work look like? Turn off the TV or the Internet and read a book. One of my favourite authors is Wayne Dyer. He speaks of love, spirituality, personal responsibility and growth.

Reading helps me to think in a way that serves me. I'm not saying you can't watch TV. God knows I still enjoy some TV, but if you only watch TV and get wrapped up in the negative dramas of reality or crime shows, it may be hurting your mental and spiritual health.

There are so many wonderful authors whose works have the power to help you. For you, it might be the Bible, uplifting fiction novels, or personal development books by authors like Wayne Dyer. The information and messages you consume eventually become your state of mind. If you already have a low state of mind from a problematic past, then watching hate-filled TV will reinforce the mental patterns you developed. Reading uplifting books helps positively rewire your brain.

Next is your body. Walk every day. Do yoga. Go to a gym every day. Science proves that regular exercise improves your brain function and state of well-being. To do the self-work, don't neglect your body.

Next is your mind. Find a therapist, mentor or spiritual guide to help you get in touch with the truth inside of you. We often believe we can do it all alone. "Perhaps when I'm all better I'll tell someone," we imagine. Outside help, perspective and support make a big difference in our lives. There's no chance I'd have experienced the growth I did without the Hoffman Process.

It's difficult to understand why we feel the way we do without help. We think we're the only ones with these feelings. We wonder why we're angry and in a state of self-hatred. We don't know why, and we feel alone, but a guide can help make sense of it all.

To know why is immensely powerful. Why has the power to set us free. I always knew my problems stemmed from my abuse and the cover-up. I'd been hurt and then silenced, but I didn't realize I hated myself until I did the Hoffman Process.

I recommend the Hoffman Process. If you can't do the Hoffman Process, please find a program involving outside help that works for you.

Strand #4 – Self-Love

Self-love follows from self-work. Loving yourself is like a garden. Unless it's diligently tended, a garden will get weedy and be over-grown.

It's sometimes thought that self-love is selfish. That's a lie. We must be able to love ourselves before we can honestly give of ourselves and help others. Self-love allows us to give freely. Why? When we are full of love, it flows out of us. Think of yourself like a teapot. The tea inside is love. To serve tea, you must have tea in the pot. If all you ever do is pour, the teapot will be empty pretty soon. You need to fill your teapot before serving others.

Helping others is an act of love. To truly help others, we must be full of love. Start by loving yourself first. Care for yourself, love yourself and then love others.

Strand #5 – Accountability

To my knowledge, nobody has ever made drastic, powerful and healthy changes without accountability.

Accountability means fessing up when something doesn't go our way, and recognizing the role we played. Accountability means acknowledging that nobody else holds the key to our happiness. Nothing else, even the death of our abuser, can heal us. We must recover from within, and we must be held accountable for that healing. It means we can't blame anyone else for it, even our abuser. It means we can't mistreat others and blame anyone else for our actions.

Accountability is robust, it's healthy and it's complicated. It's especially difficult when we've lived for several years or decades blaming others. This is a big hang-up I encounter with adult survivors. I've had adult survivors meet me and then get angry with me within a few days. They love me, and when they realize that I can't heal them, they lash out at me.

They have made a habit of blaming others for everything that happens in life. They find comfort and solace in blaming. It starts by blaming the abuser, but it soon becomes easy to blame others for everything.

There's no magic pill. Healing must come from within you. Others can throw ropes to you if you're stuck in the hole, but they can't heal you. The accountability for healing lies on each of our shoulders.

Strand #6 – Surrender

The most significant and most challenging strand of the rope for me was surrender.

All the other rope strands are about the things we can control. Most of the rope is about doing something, the kind of thing an entrepreneur like me understands. There's immense power in taking proactive steps to get better. But hard work can't help at all with surrender.

To surrender, we need to let go completely. It's like that old cliché you hear from athletes—they can only control their preparation, not the result. You can't control the outcome either. Neither can I. That is a harsh lesson to learn.

Surrender has always been the hardest step for me. I've always wanted to control every aspect of life. I've associated letting go of any element of control to be a loss. It stems from the abuse, where I had no control over anything, especially what Wib did to my body.

Little Warriors and self-awareness have taught me that total control isn't possible. Believing we control the outcome and never letting go in an attempt to force a result is a recipe for living a personal hell. It's an invitation to stress and unhappiness. When you're on your path of healing, the only option you have after doing everything within your control is to surrender. Let go and see what shows up.

Not only will great things often come to you but also they'll feel like an unexpected blessing when they do because you'll have let go of the false belief that you're in control.

I urge you to do the same with your process of healing. Take control of the process, but surrender the outcome.

Be brave. Just let go.

CHAPTER 22

I AM SURRENDER

"Sometimes when you're in a dark place you think you've been buried, but you've actually been planted."

— *Christine Caine*

No one escapes child sexual abuse without massive wounds that take a lifetime to heal.

The eight-year old girl, hiding in the dark, under a stairwell, trying to escape the terror of the monster in her grandmother's house, has come a long way. She never could have imagined all she would accomplish or the accolades that would come her way.

But, God knew.

Organizations honoured me with awards that were humbling experiences. But they also gave me a platform to share my story and raise greater awareness about child sexual abuse.

Canadian Mental Health Association (CMHA), Alberta Division 2020 Nadine Stirling Award

Meritorious Service Medal

L'Oréal Paris Women of Worth National Nominee and Honouree for 2020

Kiwanis Canada Club Citizen of the Year Award

2018 Stars of Alberta Volunteer Award

Recognition by the Alberta Government and Canadian for a Civil Society for Volunteer and Community Work

2018 Canada's Most Powerful Women – CIBC Trailblazers & Trendsetters

50 Most Outstanding Canadians

BMO Celebrating Women Award

RBC Canadian Women Entrepreneur Social Change Award

City of Edmonton Citation Award for Community Service

Queen Elizabeth II Diamond Jubilee Medal

Top 40 Canadians Under 40

Me to We Award for Social Action

Rotary Integrity Award

Ernst & Young Entrepreneur of the Year for 2009

Global Woman of Vision

YMCA Woman of Distinction

Leading the Way

In 2020, over 30,000 adults have been educated across Canada and over 400 children plus their families have attended the treatment program at the Be Brave Ranch since we opened the doors.

We have demonstrated clinical successes (as demonstrated through our outcome measures) through research with the University of Alberta.

We are a fully licensed facility with Child and Family Services. We are accredited with the Canadian Accreditation Council and are recognized as a leader in trauma-informed care.

We provide our services free of cost to families, including transportation and familial costs. We are recognized as having strong community partnerships with other governmental sectors, community stakeholders, as well as caregivers.

We are recognized clinically as a leader in trauma-informed practice and have provided education and knowledge/support/expertise to various agencies such as the Office of the Child and Youth Advocate (OCYA), Ben Calf Robe Society, Enoch Cree Nation, Youth Justice, PolicyWise, etc.

We have a Scientific and Clinical Oversite committee to ensure leading practices.

Ultimately though, we would like to work towards preventing child sexual abuse so there isn't a need to treat children who have been traumatized by sexual abuse.

Be Brave Bridge

Over 100 children and youth come to the Be Brave Ranch every year. Unfortunately, so many more are on our waiting list, and now, as a result of the COVID-19 situation, vulnerable children and teens are more isolated and at risk than ever.

For these reasons, we have developed the Be Brave Bridge Online Program. The Be Brave Bridge is a comprehensive online program that connects specialized counselors and therapists with children, teens and parents impacted by child sexual abuse who might not otherwise receive timely mental health support.

Following COVID-19, these online programs for children, teens and families will become part of our ongoing effort to help children and youth across Canada stabilize before they arrive at the Be Brave Ranch. We are also optimistic that, for some children and teens, the online program will provide them with enough strategies, skills and tools that they will not require the intensive treatment provided at the Be Brave Ranch.

Designed with significant input from many leading academic and clinical experts who specialize in child sexual abuse, the Be Brave Bridge Online Program will offer similar evidence-based, specialized trauma treatment to what's provided at the Be Brave Ranch. We've taken the insights used at the Ranch and embedded them into the Be Brave Bridge program. All of the information provided has been carefully researched and offers the most effective interventions and strategies.

It's our dream that once the Be Brave Bridge program is up and running, we will be able get it licensed and translated into all languages to help people around the world. We hope to expand our facility and be operating at full capacity. After our online program is up and running, the next goal would be to open an adult facility for survivors, a place where men and women can come together and have their voice heard.

The cost estimate of child sexual abuse in Canada exceeds $3.6 billion dollars annually. This includes both public and private costs across four policy areas: Health, social/public services, justice, education/research and employment.

Little Warriors continues to operate solely through generous donors. That's one of the reasons I'm sharing my story. Our movement needs to become stronger, bolder and sustainable.

It Was All for the Kids

The kids.

So much changed when I started to let myself be driven by the kids. I opened my heart to the possibility of change in the world around me. I changed when I surrendered, accepted the past and focused on acting out of love as my guiding principle.

It's amazing the people that come into your life when you live by these principles. Without a doubt, the kids that have been victimized by childhood sexual abuse have inspired me the most. Their plight has driven me for years now. And that has been a kind of surrender. Ever since that day in Montreal, I've known this purpose was chosen for me. It's been one long journey of surrender ever since then.

When I surrender to the purpose I've been called to accomplish, I make progress. When I fight it, or when I try to control everything myself, that's when I've faced the most significant challenges. The world does conspire to help you when you surrender to the process.

All the survivor kids have inspired me, but it's almost magical the way surrender has led me to my three little angels. I call them my Little Warriors. I don't want to overstep my bounds concerning their real families, but these three girls have become like children to me. They visit me at my home and spend holidays with me, and they have become everything to me.

Alison is the teenage survivor from Coaldale I've mentioned previously. She raised tens of thousands of dollars for the Be Brave Ranch. Alison epitomizes bravery. I've been in her shoes. I was once a teenager who experienced sexual abuse. I know how difficult it can be to come forward. That alone is a mountain to climb. Alison came forward and shared her story, and she's become a strong advocate for change and a supporter of healing and love.

I'm proud that Little Warriors has helped give her a voice to be such a strong leader and honoured that she's used her enormous energy to help us build the Ranch.

It's hard to explain the bond I feel with this girl. She's everything I would have wanted for myself at the same age. It's so incredible to witness.

Kay is another of my little angels. She's the first victor kid I ever met face to face. Like Alison, she's taken an active role in her healing. She's doing something about it, and that's why I call these kids victors. Kay was looking online one day for a place to meet other survivors and to see how she could heal and get better from her abuse. She came across some YouTube videos of me. That led her to research me and Little Warriors and all the work we were doing.

She was inspired and excited, so she wrote me a letter and sent me a bracelet. I wrote her a letter back and then she called me. That was a special moment for me. I know I was led to a much deeper state of surrender. I always did this for the kids, but when I started meeting more and more of them that surrender and sense of calling deepened.

I flew her out to meet me, and it was the beginning of a beautiful relationship. I'm grateful to meet Kay and inspired by her courage and the leadership she's shown. She's another of my Little Warriors.

Then there is Halie. She's another survivor turned victor—another of my Little Warrior angels. I won't recount it here, but the things she has experienced are horrific beyond what anyone should suffer. That makes it all the more amazing how much she is overcoming. When we were raising money for the Ranch she held lemonade stands, garage sales, and she asked for cash donations to the Ranch for her birthday rather than any gifts for herself. She raised more than $500, which is simply remarkable for a little girl.

The Ranch and this book are for those three angels and everything kids like them represent. It's for all survivors of childhood sexual abuse and the movement devoted to healing these angels. You embody everything I ever dreamed of for Little Warriors.

You are the reason I've healed. Thank you.

It was my brokenness that inspired something so special… so important.

Through building the Ranch, I've healed.

Beautifully Broken

I've discovered that all of us are beautifully broken but it is in our brokenness that we become game changers, that we make things happen because we understand darkness and we understand pain and the end of our comfort zone. The Ranch is a testament to the fact that it is in vulnerability that we can start to build beautiful things. The people, who are truly happy in their lives, are people who embrace vulnerability and share it with people whom they're close to. From one Warrior to another, live more present and allow yourself to be vulnerable.

I realized that grit is about having an "ultimate concern"—a goal you care about so much that it organizes and gives meaning to almost everything you do. And grit is holding steadfast to that goal. Even when you fall down. Even when you screw up. Even when progress toward that goal is halting or slow.

The greatest gifts I received were from places of complete darkness. I've learned to feel compassion and love for other people because I know what it is like to live in darkness. Little Warriors was a whisper from God in the darkness. If you are quiet enough, you can hear God's whisper and that is the work that God calls you to do. I never chose this path; it chose me. I am a broken girl who did something good because God asked me to do it. It is only with God's love that I was able to walk with him on this journey. Listen, especially in the darkness, for your purpose. You are never alone.

Over the years following the opening of the Ranch, I would need to draw from everything I'd learned and my trusted circle of family and friends to make it through an economic recession, a life and death battle with cancer and the resulting PTSD and depression.

Make no mistake—childhood sexual abuse is not something I've gotten over or moved beyond. Truly, I feel the effects of the abuse in my life every day. Thirty-nine years after the torment, I still don't have everything together. Writing this book reminded me that in many ways I am forced to be silent. There are facts and details that I cannot publicly disclose. My trust was betrayed, my innocence was stolen from me, I lost my family, my scars are invisible yet deep, I seldom feel like I'm enough and I worry that I'm not lovable.

My team describes me as "beautifully crazy."

But, I've done the work. If you're facing the effects of childhood sexual abuse, I hope my story has helped convince you that you will get better. Do the work. Apply what you've read about forgiveness and love. Choose to surrender. Control is a myth. The control you have is to choose your attitude and perspective. You will get better. You will build resiliency and strength. You will become a warrior.

The conclusion of this book is not the end of my story. There are more stories, including ones I have yet to live. Will the future be easy?

I know it won't be easy but it will be worth it.

And I know I can get there now because… I am a Warrior.

APPENDIX

Little Warriors is a national, charitable organization committed to the awareness, prevention and treatment of child sexual abuse. We also advocate on behalf of and with child sexual abuse survivors.

Our Mission

- Raise awareness and provide information about child sexual abuse.

- Advocate to ensure the rights, needs and interests of children are respected and protected.

- Provide child sexual abuse prevention strategies to adults through education.

- Provide a treatment facility to help children cope with the devastating effects of child sexual abuse.

Experts estimate that 1 in 3 girls and 1 in 6 boys will experience sexual abuse. (1) Sadly, 95% of those children will know and trust their perpetrator (2) and even more alarming is that 95% of child sexual abuse cases go unreported (3).

Founded by Glori Meldrum in 2008, Little Warriors currently offers a free workshop called Prevent It! Taking Action to Stop Child Sexual Abuse to educate adults across Canada on how to help prevent child sexual abuse. Researchers at the University of Alberta developed the evidence-based education workshop and research shows it significantly improves attitudes, knowledge and behaviour. (4) This workshop is unique in Canada and was developed using research-informed methods and evaluated with scientific rigour.

The Little Warriors Be Brave Ranch is located east of Edmonton and is the first of its' kind long-term, evidence-based, trauma informed treatment centre for children ages 8-16 who have been sexually abused. With over 200 hours of multimodal therapy for the children and families over the course of a year, the Be Brave Ranch gives child sexual abuse survivors the essential support they need to grow into happy, healthy adults. Clinical results confirm the success of the treatment program including an almost 50% reduction in child Post-Traumatic Stress Disorder scores (PTSD), a reduction in the number of children experiencing PTSD, significant reductions in Depression and Anxiety, an improvement in Self-esteem and cognitive abilities and forecasts that also suggest reduced mental health related issues and enriched outcomes for these children and society in the future. (5, 6, 7)

To make a donation or for more information about Little Warriors and the Be Brave Ranch please visit littlewarriors.ca

For a list of resources, reading recommendations, statistics and research related to child sexual abuse visit littlewarriors.ca

Reading Recommendations, Statistics and Research

(1) Child Sexual Abuse (The Canadian Badgley Royal Commission, Report on Sexual Offences Against Children and Youths), 1984. (Pg. 175)

(2) Child Sexual Abuse (The Canadian Badgley Royal Commission, Report on Sexual Offences Against Children and Youths), 1984. (Pg. 215-218)

(3) An Evidence-Based Education Program for Adults about Child Sexual Abuse ("Prevent It!") That Significantly Improves Attitudes, Knowledge, and Behavior Martin and Silverstone

(4) How Much Child Sexual Abuse is "Below the Surface," and Can We Help Adults Identify it Early? Martin & Silverstone

(5) Design of a Comprehensive One-Year Program at the Be Brave Ranch to help Children who have been Victims of Sexual Abuse Peter H Silverstone, Farrel Greenspan, Millie Silverstone, Hanelle Sawa

(6) A Complex Multimodal 4-Week Residential Treatment Program Significantly Reduces PTSD Symptoms in Child Sexual Abuse Victims: The Be Brave Ranch Peter H Silverstone, Farrel Greenspan, Millie Silverstone, Hanelle Sawa

(7) Cognitive Improvements in Child Sexual Abuse Victims Occur Following Multimodal Treatment Program: As Measured by MyCognition Quotient Matthew Reeson, Andrew J Greenshaw, Vincent Agyapong, Gary Hnatko, Hannah Pazderka, Wanda Polzin and Peter H Silverstone

Published Articles Related to the BBR Program in the Journal of Child & Adolescent Behaviour

1. Design of a Comprehensive One-Year Program at the Be Brave Ranch to help Children who have been Victims of Sexual Abuse

https://www.omicsonline.org/open-access/design-of-a-comprehensive-oneyear-program-at-the-be-brave-ranch-to-help-children-who-have-been-victims-of-sexual-abuse-2375-4494.1000180.pdf

2. A Complex Multimodal 4-Week Residential Treatment ProgramSignificantly Reduces PTSD Symptoms in Child Sexual Abuse Victims: The Be Brave Ranch

https://www.omicsonline.org/open-access/a-complex-multimodal-4week-residential-treatment-program-significantlyreduces-ptsd-symptoms-in-child-sexual-abuse-victims-the-be-b-2375-4494-1000275.pdf

3. Cognitive Improvements in Child Sexual Abuse Victims Occur Following Multimodal Treatment Program: As Measured by My-Cognition Quotient

https://www.omicsonline.org/open-access/cognitive-improvements-in-child-sexual-abuse-victims-occur-following-multimodal-treatment-program-as-measured-by-mycogni.pdf

4. A Novel 2-week Intensive Multimodal Treatment Program for Child Sexual Abuse (CSA) Survivors is Associated with Mental Health Benefits for Females aged 13-16

https://www.cacap-acpea.org/wp-content/uploads/A-Novel-2-week-Intensive-Multimodal-Treatment-Program.pdf

ABOUT THE AUTHOR

Glori Meldrum is a career entrepreneur. Together with her husband, Gary, she founded, and manages g[squared], one of Alberta's top strategic business and commercial marketing firms. The Meldrums are philanthropists and devoted parents of four children. Glori is involved in a number of projects for local not-for-profit organizations including Adeara, Grit, The Stollery Children's Hospital Foundation and WinHouse.

Glori is a survivor of child sexual abuse and an impassioned crusader against child sexual abuse. The non-profit organization she founded, Little Warriors, is the driving force for healing survivors and preventing child sexual abuse.

The Be Brave Ranch is the first trauma-informed treatment centre in the world for children who have been sexually abused. It opened in 2014. The Ranch is the culmination of Glori's seven-year mission to show how she transformed her pain into healing. The Ranch was built entirely by volunteers and generous donations from Alberta-based companies and individuals. Glori's contagious passion attracted some of the finest clinicians, researchers and business leaders. Working together, they developed a world-class treatment centre. In its first six years of operation the innovative, multi-modal, trauma-informed therapies produced remarkable results in children. PTSD, Depression and Anxiety were reduced 50% in child survivors aged 8-12. Building on this success, the first cohort of girls, ages 13-16, was initiated in October 2018.

Glori's hard work hasn't gone unnoticed. Glori was among the top 18 finalists from 6,400 nominees for the 2017 RBC Entrepreneur of the Year Award for Social Change for her work with Little Warriors. She was the recipient of the 2011 Canadian Living Me to We Award—Social Action category; Ernst & Young's Entrepreneur of the Year award in the Social Entrepreneur category; the 2009 Rotary Integrity Award; a 2008 Global Woman of Vision award; a 2005 YWCA Woman of Distinction award; named one of Caldwell Partners' 2010 "Top 40 Canadians Under 40"; the first female president of the Entrepreneur's Organization (EO) of Edmonton; Alberta Shining Star Award; the L'Oreal Paris Woman of Worth award; and she is listed in the top 100 most powerful women in Canada.

IN APPRECIATION

Zander Robertson helped me get my story down on paper in 2015. He captured my memories and emotions in black and white. I am forever indebted to Zander for starting the writing process.

Bob Jones of REVwords.com was a part of my first Little Warriors advertising campaign in 2008. Bob believes in the power of my story and helped bring my story alive in my own voice.

Thank you to Brad Ray of Minuteman Press for your generosity in printing the book.

Manufactured by Amazon.ca
Bolton, ON

18379546R00146